The QUR'AN
&
The BIBLE
In The Light Of
Science

The QUR'AN
&
The BIBLE
In The Light Of
Science

A Rejoinder to
Dr. William Campbell's
comments

Dr. Zakir Naik

Edited by
A. R. Uganwi

The Qur'an & the Bible in the light of Science

Dr. Zakir Naik

Edited by **A. R. Uganwi**

First Edition – 2008

Published by Abdul Naeem for

Islamic Book Service

2872-74, Kucha Chelan, Darya Ganj,
New Delhi - 110 002 (India)
Ph.: +91-11-23253514, 23286551, 23244556
Fax: +91-11-23277913, 23247899
E-mail: islamic@eth.net/ ibsdelhi@del2.vsnl.net.in
visit us at: www.islamicindia.in/ www.islamicindia.co.in

Our Associates

- Al-Munna Book Shop Ltd. **(UAE)**
  (Sharjah) *Tel.:* 06-561-5483, 06-561-4650
  (Dubai) *Tel.:* 04-352-9294

- Azher Academy Ltd., **London (UK)**
  Tel.: 020-8911-9797

- Lautan Lestari (Lestari Books), **Jakarta (Indonesia)**
  Tel.: 0062-21-35-23456

- Husami Book Depot, **Hyderabad (India)**
  Tel.: 0406680-6285

Printed in India

CONTENTS

Introduction

After our beloved Prophet (S.A.W.), it is his Ummah's responsibility to invite the people towards the fold of Islam. *Alhamdulillah*, there is no dearth of the *Da'yees* who have wholeheartedly devoted themselves to the self-assigned task of disseminating the virtues of Islam with whatever *modus-operandi* they find better as per the situation prevailing or depending upon the need of the hour.

However, this is the period entirely different from the period of the complete ignorance or *daur-e-jahiliya*. Before the advent of Islam, various evils were prevalent, especially in the Arabian Peninsula, because they were completely ignorant of Islam, and even obstinate to accept the goodness taught and exhorted by the earlier prophets (Peace be upon them). But today, the people are more wise and educated. They study and understand many aspects of their belief, yet they hesitate to accept the virtues and principles of Islam, because they have a misconception that Islam is a harsh religion, spread on the edges of sword.

Such misconceptions have carved out a niche in the hearts of the Non-Muslims, because they are either ignorant of the Islamic teachings or they are yet to be taught and convinced with authentic scriptural references, proofs and the logic required to apply for their better understanding as well as acceptance.

If the Non-Muslims are simply invited to embrace Islam only with the persuasive words, describing that the Qur'an and the Hadith say to accept this Divine religion, and so they must accept or embrace it; they would simply raise the question, what is the logic behind it and why should they not continue to follow the faith of their forefathers?

6

And then, arises the need to teach them the Islamic virtues — the Dos & Don'ts of Islam in a thoroughly comparative perspective. So, the best way to acquaint them with the religion of Islam is by shedding light on their own religious scriptures and their ongoing practices in comparison with the Qur'anic teachings as well as those of the *Hadith*.

If a Hindu is approached with the *Da'wah* of Islam, he is to be taught Islam first by dispelling his misconceptions about this divine religion and simultaneously, he should also be acquainted with the sayings of their own religious scriptures, depending upon the religions they follow.

Similarly, if a *da'yee* wants to approach a Christian with the invitation of Islam, he should teach him also with the relevant references of their sacred book, the Bible in comparison with the Qur'an and the *Hadith* as also with the required logic if the situation demands for the same. So, the need of the time is that a *da'yee* of Islam should be well versed not only in Islam but also with the religion, whose followers are to be preached by him.

Alhamdulillah, in the bevy of some renowned *da'yees* Dr. Zakir Abdul Karim Naik, popularly known as Dr. Zakir Naik is not only the man of the distinct scholarly feats but also a global figure of repute and accomplishments in the field of Islamic Da'wah. He is the President of **Islamic Research Foundation**, Mumbay, India. Though a medical doctor by professional training, he is well known as a dynamic international orator in Islam as well as Comparative Religion. He clarifies Islamic viewpoints and dispels the misconceptions about Islam, based upon the Qur'an, Hadith and the other religious scriptures, besides adhering to reason, logic and scientific facts.

7

Dr. Zakir Naik has been proved a perfect scholar and da'yee to answers the questions showered by the carping critics of Islam in a way they want and then, they remain unable to give gruff remarks because they are explained with the relevant and authentic references besides the logic applicable there.

Today, there are several Non-Muslims, who want the proofs of Islamic teachings in the light of Science. If they are taught that there are many inventions and discoveries, made 1400 years ago with the advent of Islam or with the revelation of the Qur'an, they try to repudiate them, claiming that these are the contributions of the modern science and the scientists.

Considering such aspects with required priority, a debate was organised in America on behalf of the organisers of the Islamic Circle of North America (ICNA) by conducting a dialogue session as well as a question-answer session on the topic **'The Qur'an and the Bible : In the light of Science'**.

This dialogue was held in a spirit of strengthening friendship and understanding each other's viewpoints. For that day's unique dialogue — the two main moderators were Dr. Mohammed Naik representing Dr. Zakir Naik, and Dr. Samuel Naaman representing Dr. William Campbell, who did his medical work in Cleveland, Ohio at Casewestern Reserve University. He worked for twenty years in Morocco, where he learnt Arabic. After 7 years in Tunisia, he wrote his book, **'Answering Dr. Maurice Bucaille'**. He is a convinced Christian, who likes to explain the *Injeel* or the Gospel to everyone; however, the present Bible is different from the *Injeel*. Before the beginning of the speakers' speeches on the selected topic, Dr. Syed Sabeel Ahmed of the ICNA greeted and welcomed all — the chief guest, honourable speakers and the audience

8

present in the hall. He assured that it was his duty to ensure a fair and proper conduct of that meeting. Therefore, he requested the speakers as well as the audience to maintain due decorum for a healthy dialogue and then the Question & Answer Session.

Thus, the dialogue session started with the turn of the speakers, Dr. William Campbell and Dr. Zakir Naik, who spoke on the particular topic selected for the debate or discussion, and made the programme not only interesting but also useful and eye-opening to all.

The particular programme consisting of dialogue and question & answer session sufficed to acquaint the Non-Muslims with the virtues of Islam, importance and utility of the Holy Qur'an and Hadith and simultaneously, they also unravelled many facts and fictions about the present Bible and the practices in vogue today among the Christians.

In a nutshell, it was Dr. Zakir Naik's rejoinder to Dr. William Campbell in dispelling many misconceptions about Islam in relation to the established science as also in acquainting the people with the present Bible, which is not, in fact, the *Injeel* which the Muslims believe as the sacred book descended upon Jesus Christ (pbuh).

THE QUR'AN & THE BIBLE IN THE LIGHT OF SCIENCE

After greeting the speakers, the chief guest and the audience, Dr. Sabeel Ahmed requested Samuel Naaman to invite the first speaker, Dr. William Campbell to speak on the particular topic selected for discussion within the stipulated period of time (turnwise) he was given. And thus, Dr. William Campbell starts with saying:

Greetings to Dr. Naik, to Sabeel Ahmed, Mohammed Naik, and greetings to the organising committee as well as to you, the audience. Calling this... 'The ultimate dialogue' will be a bit of an exaggeration, but it is a good advertising. I would like to bring greetings also in the name of Yehowah or better known as Jehowah the great Creator God, who loves us.

I wish to start by speaking about words. Tonight, we are going to speak about the words of the Bible and the words of the Qur'an. The scholars of modern linguistics tell us... 'A word, a phrase or a sentence means what it meant to the speaker, and the person or crowd of the people listening. In the case of the Qur'an, what it meant to Mohammed and those listening to him. In the case of the Bible, what it meant to Moses or Jesus, or those listening to them. To check this, we have the context of all the usage in the Bible or the Qur'an. In addition, there is the poetry and letters of that century as for the Gospel, the first century A.D and for the Qur'an, the 1st century of the *Hijra*.

DIFFERENT MEANINGS OF THE WORD, 'PIG'

If we are going to follow the truth, we may not make up new meanings. If we are seriously after truth, there are no permissible lies. Here is an example of what I am talking about. We can have the first slide here. This is talking about two dictionaries that I have in my home - One from 1951 and other from 1991. In these two dictionaries, the first meaning of the word, 'pig' is 'a young swine of either sex' — is the same. The second meaning is 'any swine or hog', 'any wild or domestic swine' — It is the same. The third is 'the flesh of swine... pork' — it is the same. Then the meaning of this particular word is 'a person or the animals of piggish habits'. It is the same... 'A person who is gluttonous.' And down here, pouring metal into a pit for pig iron, is the same. But over here, is a new meaning, which is 'A police officer'. We call police officers 'pigs.'

The question is – 'In the Torah, it is said that you cannot eat pigs. Or can I turn around and say... 'O yes! That means you cannot eat police officers.' In the Qur'an, Allah says: 'You cannot eat pigs.' Can I translate it as 'Cannot eat police officers?' No! It is wrong. It would be stupid; it would be lying actually. Mohammed did not mean 'police officers' or Moses did not mean 'police officers.' We may not have any new meanings. We must use the meanings known in the first century A.D. for the Bible or which is for the Gospel, and the first century of the Hijra for the Qur'an.

MEANING OF THE WORD, 'ALAQA' IN RELIGIOUS SCRIPTURES

Now let's look at what the Qur'an says about 'Embryology.' Oh sorry! I've got the wrong thing. It's been said that the idea of the embryo developing through stages, is a modern one. And the Qur'an is anticipating modern embryology by depicting different stages. In his pamphlet entitled **'Highlights of Human Embryology'**, by Dr. Keith Moore, he claims, 'The realisation of

11

the embryo develops in stages in the uterus was not discussed to illustrate it until the 15th century.' We will weigh this claim by considering the meaning of the Arabic words used in the Qur'an, and secondly, by examining the historical situation leading up to and surrounding the Qur'an.

We will start by looking at the main words using the word 'Alaqa' – the main verses. The Arabic word 'Alaqa' in the singular or 'Alaq' as the collective plural is used six times. In the Surah of 'The Resurrection' — 'AL-Qayamat', 75:35 to 39, we read… *'Was he man, not a drop of sperm ejaculated, then he became 'Alaqa', and God shaped and formed, and made of him a pair – the male and the female.'* In the Surah of 'The Believer' – Al Momin, 40:67, it says… *'He it is who created you from dust, then from a sperm drop, then from a leech like clot - 'Alaqa.' Then brings you forth as a child, that perhaps you may understand'*. In the Surah of 'The Pilgrimage' – Al-Hajj, 22:5, it says… *'O mankind! If you have doubt about the resurrection, consider that we have created you from dust. Then from a drop of seed, then from a clot 'Alaqa', then from a little lump of flesh, shapely and shapeless'*. And finally the following statement is there in the Surah of 'The Believers', Al-Mominun, 23:12 to 14, which reads… *'Verily, We created man from a product of wet earth, then placed him as a drop of seed in a safe lodging. Then We fashioned the drop of clot - 'Alaqa', and of the clot, We fashioned a lump, and of the lump We fashioned bones, and We clothed the bones with meat. Then We produced it as another creation'*. And here, you have the stages according to the Qur'an… 'Nutfa'— 'sperm', 'Alaqa' — 'clot', 'Mudgha'— 'piece of meat',

12

'*Azaam*'— 'bones', and the fifth stage is 'dressing the bones with muscles.

Over the last hundred plus years, the word '*Alaqa*' has been translated as follows. There are ten translations here; I am not going to read them all. Among them, 3 are in French or a 'clot of blood', 3 versions... 5 versions are in English, where it is either 'clot' or 'a leech like clot', 1 version is in Indonesian, at the bottom there... '*Siganpaudara*' —'lump clot' or 'a clot of blood' and the last one is Parsi – '*Khunbasfa*'— 'a clot of blood'.

As every reader who has studied human reproduction would realise that there is no stage, as a 'clot' during the formation of a fetus. So this is a very major scientific problem. In the dictionary it is a word, and the only meanings given for '*Alaqa*' in this feminine singular are 'clot' and 'leech'; and in North Africa, both of these meanings are still used.

Many patients have come to me to ask for a clot to be removed from their throat, and many women have come to me, complaining that their period did not come. When I say, 'I am sorry, I cannot give you medicine to bring your period, because I believe that there is a baby.' They would say, '*Mazaaltem*'— It is still blood.' So, they were understanding these ideas of the Qur'an.

Lastly, we must consider the first verses, which came to Mohammed in Mecca. These are found in the 96th Surah called '*Alaqa*' from the very word, which we are studying. In 96: 1, 2, we read... '*Proclaim in the name of your Lord, who created. Created man from 'Alaq*'. Here, the word is in the collective form. This form of the word can have other meanings, because '*Alaq*' has also been derived from the verbal noun of the word '*Alaqa*'. The verbal noun usually corresponds to 'dejerant',

13

in English as in a sense ... 'Swimming is fun'. Therefore, we could expect it to mean hanging or clinging or adhering. But the ten translators listed above have all used 'clot' or 'congealed blood' in this verse too.

In spite of the number and qualifications of these translators who used the word 'clot', the French Doctor, Maurice Bucaille has sharped the words for them. He writes ... 'What is more likely to mislead the enquiring reader, is once again the problem of vocabulary?' The majority of translations describe - for example, man's formation from a blood clot. A statement of this kind is totally unacceptable to Scientists specialising in the field. This shows how great the importance of an association between linguistic and scientific knowledge is, when it comes to grasping the meaning of the Qur'anic statements on reproduction.

Put in other words, Bucaille says, 'Nobody has translated the Qur'an correctly until I, Dr. Bucaille came along.' How does Dr. Bucaille think that it should be translated? He proposes that instead of 'clot', the word 'Alaqa' should be translated as 'something which clings', which would refer to the fetus being attached to the uterus through the placenta. But as all you ladies who have been pregnant now, the thing that clings does not stop its clinging to become chewed meat. It keeps on being a thing that clings, which is attached by the placenta for 8 and a half months. Thirdly, these verses say that... 'The chewed meat becomes bones, and then the bones are covered with muscles'.

They give the impression that first the skeleton is formed and then it is clothed with flesh — And Dr. Bucaille knows perfectly well that this is not true. The muscles and the cartilage processes of the bones start forming from the solmite at the same time. At the end

14

of the 8th week, there are only a few centres of calcification started, but the fetus is already able to make muscular movement. In a personal letter from Dr. T.W. Sadler, who is associate Professor in Embryo Anatomy and the author of 'Langman's Medical Embryology', states: 'At the eighth week post perozation, the ribs would be cartilaginous; not the bones and muscles will be present'. Also at this time, calcification will just begin. Muscles would be capable of some movement at the 8th week. It is always better to have two witnesses, so we shall see what Dr. Keith Moore has to say about the development of bones and muscles in his book 'The Developing Human'.

Extracted from the Chapters 15 and 17, we find the following information: The skeletal system develops from mesoderm. The limb muscles develop in the limb buds that are derived from this somatic mesoderm. We see that here on this slide, it is difficult perhaps to see, but there is the limb bud, and then there is just the little bit of cartilage with the muscles around. Here, there is more cartilage, and this is the whole bud. The bones are formed and in the form of bones, but it is all cartilage — No bones yet.

The second slide shows how it forms. Here is the cartilage. Though it is just the bone, it looks like cartilage, and then it starts to have some calcium deposited, and then it starts to have calcification and bone formed.

As the bone marrow is formed, mild blast develops a large muscle mass in each limb bud, separating into extensive reflexive muscles. In other words, the limb muscles develop simultaneously, for the mezincaine surrounding the developing bones. So there is the cartilage, and here are the muscles developing around the cartilage.

15

During a personal conversation with Dr. Moore, I showed him Dr. Salder's statement, and he agreed that it was absolutely valid.

CONCLUSION:

Dr. Salder and Dr. Moore agree — There is no time when calcified bones have been formed, and then the muscles are placed around them. The muscles are there, several weeks before there are calcified bones, rather than being added around previously formed bones, as the Qur'an states. The Qur'an is in complete error here. The problems are far from being solved.

Let's return to the '*Alaqa*'. Dr. Moore also has a suggestion as he says... 'Another Verse, in the Qur'an refers to the leech like appearance, and the chewed like stages of human development'. From this definition, Dr. Moore has gone ahead to propose... 'There are 23-30 days — a 23 day's embryo – 3 millimetres long that is an 8th of an inch. I can hardly put my fingers there lose together without touching. This is stage 10, shown on the inside cover of Moore's book. This is the beginning, and here is the sperm entering the egg — So that is stage 1.

Comes down here to stage 6th in the second week, and here is the 3rd week. And there is the first stage 10, and here is day 23, and this is what Dr. Moore wants to say... 'Looks like a leech'. If we could look further though, and look at the x-ray, here is the day 22 and the backbone is still open. And when we look at day 23, the backbone is open there and the head is wide open. It does not look like a leech at all. And if you keep on, this is the diagram of it. The head is open, the nogstral neurropore, and finally this diagram shows there is the 20 day embryo. It has got a yolk sac, it has got an umbilicus; it does not look like a leech at all.

16

The great problem with these two definitions for the word '*Alaqa*' is that no confirming examples have been provided from the Arabic used.

In the centuries surrounding the Hijri, the only way to establish the meaning of the word is by usage. The only way to establish whether the singular form '*Alaqa*' can mean a 3 millimetres 'embryo' or 'the thing that clings' is to bring the census, demonstrating this usage from the letter, throughout the Arabs of Mecca and Medina, close to the time of Mohammed, especially from the language of the Quraish. This will not be an easy task because much work has already been done on the clear Arabic of the Quraish. The early Muslims understood intuitively the need to know exactly what the Qur'anic words mean — And for this reason, they make comprehensive studies of their language and poetry.

Hence, Abu Bakr, the former Rector of 'The Main Mask in 'pairs' brought up this subject at a conference, under one God in Munkalia, 1985. He posed the question to the audience... 'Has the comprehend of the text of the Qur'an, known at the time of Mohammed remained stable?' And his answer was... 'Ancient poetry shows that it has'. We can only conclude... 'If the verses which bring spiritual comfort and hope to Muslims have remained stable, then the scientific statements embedded in those Verses must also be accepted as stable unless new evidence can be brought forward'. This is especially important, since some of the verses say that this information is a sign.

The Surah of 'The Believers' we saw above, says: '*He it is, who created you from dust, then from a sperm drop, then from a clot...* 'Alaqa' that perhaps you may understand'. And in the Surah of 'The Pilgrimage', He said: 'O Mankind! If you have doubt about the resurrection, consider…'. Therefore, the question must be asked… 'If it was a clear sign to the men and women of Mecca and Medina, what did they understand from the word 'Alaqa' which would lead them to faith in the resurrection?' The answer is 'We are going to examine the historical situation leading up to the time of Mohammed, to see what Mohammed and his people believed about embryology'.

THE STAGES OF EMBRYOLOGY ACCORDING TO APOCRITIES

We will start with Apocrities. According to the best evidence, he was born on the Greek Island of Kuss in 460 B.C. and he has stages. His stages are as follows - The sperm is a product, which comes from the whole body of each parent - Weak sperm coming from the weak parts and strong sperm from the strong parts. Then he goes ahead and talks about the coagulation of the mother's blood. The seed embryo is then contained in the membrane. Moreover it grows because of its mother's blood, which descends to the womb. For once a woman conceives she ceases to menstruate.

Then about flesh, he says: 'At this stage, with the descend in coagulation of the mother's blood, flesh begins to be formed with the umbilicus, and lastly the bones. He says: 'As the flesh grows, it is formed in this distinct members by breath. The bones grow hard, and send out into branches like a tree.

Aristotle's Point of view regarding the Stages of Embryology.

Next, we will look at Aristotle. In his book on the generation of animals, sometime about 350 B.C, he gives his stages of embryology and he talks about 'first semen' and 'menstrual blood' or 'catemania'. In this section, Aristotle speaks of the male semen

18

as being in a pure state. It follows, that what the female would contribute to the semen of the male, would be material for the semen to work on. In other words, the semen clots the menstrual blood, and then it goes to flesh. He say⌐ that nature forms this from the purest material... 'the flesh' and from the residue there are, which forms bones. And lastly around the flesh around the bones, and attached to them by thin fibrous bands, grow the fleshly parts. Clearly, the Qur'an follows this exactly. Sperm clotting in the menstrual blood, which forms meat. Thereafter, the bones are formed and lastly around about the bones grow the fleshly parts.

THE STAGES OF EMBRYOLOGY IN THE LIGHT OF THE INDIAN MEDICAL SCIENCE

Next we will consider the Indian medicine. The opinion of Sharaka in 123 A.D. and Shushruta is that... 'Both — the male and female contributed seed. The secretion of the male is called the *sukra*—semen. The secretion of the woman is called the *Artava*—sanita... blood. And it is derived from the blood by way of food, by way of blood'. Here, we see that in the medicine of India, they too had the idea that the child was formed from semen and blood.

THE STAGES OF EMBRYOLOGY ACCORDING TO GALEN

Now we shall look at Galen, who was born in 131 A.D, in Bergamum. Modern Bergamum is in Turkey. Galen says... 'Semen, the substance from which the fetus is formed, is not merely menstrual blood, as Aristotle maintained, but menstrual blood plus the two semen.

The Qur'an agrees with Galen here, when it says in Surah 76:2, *'We created man from a drop of mingled sperm'*. Now we look at the Galen stages. Galen also taught that the embryo develops in stages. The first is that, in which the form of the semen prevails. The next stage is when it has been filled with blood, and heart and brain and liver are still unarticulated and unshaped. This is the period that Hippocrates called 'fetus'.

The Qur'anic Surah 22:5 reflects this saying, *'Then out of a morsel of flesh, partly formed and partly unformed. And* now *the third period of gestation has come. Thus, this nature caused flesh to grow on and around all the bones'*. We saw above that the Qur'an agrees with this. In Surah 23:14, where it says: *'And We clothe the bones with meat'*.

The fourth and final period is at the stage when all the parts in the limbs get differentiated. Galen was so important in medicine that just about the time of the Hijra, 4 leading medical men in Alexandria, Egypt, decided to form a Medical School, using 16 books of Galen as the basis of the studies. This continued up to, and including the 13th century. We must now ask ourselves — What was the political, economic and medical situation in Arabia at the time of Mohammed?

From the Hajra Mount in Yemen, the caravans of the spice trade past North through Mecca and Medina, and then reached into all of Europe. In North Arabia, in about 500 A.D, the Gazaneeds took over, and by 528, they controlled the Syrian deserts over to the outskirts of Medina. 'Syraic'... a form of Aramaic related to Arabic, was their official language. As early as 463, the Jews translated the Torah and Old Testament from Hebrew into 'Syriac' — The British Museum has a copy.

This was made available to the Guscians, who were Christians and to the Jewish tribes in Arabia. During this time Syrgius Cyrra

Cynie who died in Constantinople in 536, one of the earliest and greatest translators from Greek into Syraic, who translated various works on medicine, including 26 works of Galen. This made them available in the kingdom of Kasrov-I in Persia and to the Ghasan tribe, whose influence extended, to the outskirts of Medina. Kasrov I, Arabic Kisra, King of Persia was known as Kasrov the great. His troops conquered areas as far away as Yemen. He also loved learning and started several schools. The school of Jundi Shapueer became during Kasrov first's long reign of 48 years — The greatest intellectual centre of the time. Within it's walls Greek, Jewish, Nostorian, Persian and Hindu thoughts and experience were freely exchanged. Teaching was done largely in Syriac — from Syraic translations of Greek texts. This method Aristotle, Hypocrates and Galen were readily available when the Medical School of Jundi Shapueer was operating during his reign.

The next step was that the conquering Arabs compelled the Nostorians to translate their Cyriac text of Greek medicine into Arabic. The translation from Syriac to Arabic was easy, as the two languages had the same grammar. Considering the local medical situation during Mohammed's life, we know there were physicians living in Arabia during this period.

Harith bin Caladia was the best-educated physician trained in the healing art. He was born about the middle of the 6th century at Taif in the tribe of Bani Sakif. He travelled through Yemen and then Persia where he received his education in the Medical Sciences at the great Medical School of Jundi Shapueer. And thus, he was intimately acquainted with the medical teachings of Aristotle, Hypocrates and Galen. Having completed his studies, he practised as a Physician in Persia, and during that time he was called to the court of King Kasrov with whom he had a long conversation. He came back to Arabia about the beginning of Islam, and settled down at Taif.

While there, Abu Khair, a King of Yemen came to see Harith in connection with a certain diseases and on being cured, he rewarded him with much money and a slave girl. Though Harith bin Caladia did not write any book on Medicine, his views on many medical problems are still preserved in his conversation with Kasrov.

About the eye, Harith says that it constituted of 'fat', which is the white spot. About the second is constituted with 'water', which is the black part. And of 'wind' which constitutes the eyesight. All these things we know to be wrong now, but this was Greek thought. All it goes to show the acquaintance of Harith with the Greek doctors.

Summarising the situation in a few words in his book, **'Eastward delamitry Arabs'**, Dr. Lucaine La' Clerk writes…Harith bin Caladia studied medicine in Jundi Shapueer, and Mohammed owed to Harith the part of his medical knowledge. Thus, with the one as well as the other, we easily recognise the traces of Greek medicine. Sometimes Mohammed treated the sick, but in the difficult cases he would send the patients to Harith. Another educated person around Mohammed was Laden bin Harith. Not related to the doctor, he was a Pershiate and cousin of Mohammed, and had also visited the court of Kasrov. He had learned Persian and music, which he introduced among the Quraish at Mecca. However, he was not sympathetic to Mohammed — Marking some of the stories in the Qur'an. Mohammed never forgave him for this, and when he was taken prisoner in the battle of Badr, he caused him to be put to death.

In summary, we see that 1) the Arabs living in Mecca and Medina in 600, had political and economical relations with people from Ethiopia, Yemen, Persia and Byzantine. 2) A cousin of Mohammed knew Persian well enough to do his musical studies in it. 3) The Ghasine tribe, which ruled the Syrian Desert over to the gates of Medina, used Syriar, one of the main languages used to teach medicine — And Jundi Shapueer is their official language.

An ill king of Yemen came to Taif to consult the physician, Harith Bin Caladia, who had been trained well at Jundi Shapueer – the best medical school in that world, and to whom Mohammed sometimes send patients.

5) During Mohammed's lifetime a new medical school was established in Alexandria, using the 16 books of Galen as their text. This source shows that there was ample opportunity for Mohammed and the people around him to have heard the embryological theories of Aristotle, Apocratis and Galen, when they went to seek treatment from Harith bin Caladia and other local doctors. Thus, when the Qur'an says in the late Meccan Surah of 'The Believer', 40: 67…'*He it is who created you from dust, then from a sperm drop, then from a leach like clot, that perhaps you may understand'. And then in the Surah of 'The Pilgrimage'… 'O! Mankind! If you have doubt about the resurrection, consider that we have created you from dust'.*

It is correct for us to ask again, what were they to understand? What were they to consider? And here are the Qur'anic stages again – Nutfa—'sperm', *Alaqa*—'clot', *Mudgha*— 'piece of meat', Azaam—bones. And… 5) dressing of bones with muscles.'

23

The answer is very clear. They were understanding and considering that which was common knowledge, the embryological stages as taught by the Greek physicians.

I don't mean that Mohammed's listeners all knew the names of the Greek physicians, but they knew the embryological stages acknowledged by the Greek physicians. They believed that the male sperm mixed with the female menstrual blood to cause it to clot, and this became the baby. 2) They believed there was a time when the fetus was formed, and unformed. 3) They believed the bones formed first, and then was covered with muscles. Allah was using that common knowledge as a sign, encouraging the listeners and readers to turn to Him. The trouble is that this common knowledge was and is not true.

After the era of physicians after Mohammed, we must now look at two well-known Physicians. Obviously, they had no effect on the Qur'an, but they demonstrated that the faith and the embryological ideas of Aristotle, Apocrates and Galen continued among the Arabs right up to the sixteen hundreds. If the correct translation of *Alaqa* is 'leach-like substance' as modern Muslims like Shabbir Ali claims, there is no place for these post Qur'anic doctors who said so. In fact, it is just the opposite.

The ideas of these Greek Physicians were being used to explain the Qur'an, which was coded to enlighten the meaning of the Greek Physicians. The human being takes its origin from two. - This is speaking about Evenesena or Avisena. The human being takes its origin from two things – the male sperm, which plays the part of factor – the female sperm... first part of the menstrual blood, which provides the matter. Thus, we see that Ibn Seena gave the female semen, exactly the same role that Aristotle has

24

assigned to the menstrual blood. It is difficult to overstate the importance of Ibn Seena as a scientific and philosophical authority for the pre-modern Europeans.

Then we are going to look at Ibn Khaima Zaujia. Ibn Khaima took full advantage of the agreement between the Qur'anic Revelation and Greek medicine. It is not very clear probably, but the Hippocrates is in purplish, and the Qur'an is in bold type green, and the Hadith is in purple, and commentaries are in red, and his own thoughts, in sort of a blue-green.

So it starts out – He is giving - He says Hippocrates said, in the third Ch. of Kitab al-Ajinna.…'The semen is contained in a membrane, and it grows because of the blood of its mother, which descends to the womb. Some membranes are formed at the beginning, others after the second month and others in the third month'. And this phrase about the blood descending to the womb, we saw it when we looked at Hippocrates slide. That is why God said here in the Qur'an which is mentioned as…*'He creates you in the womb of your mothers, by one formation after another, in three darkness' - That is the Qur'an 39:6.*

Then he gives his own ideas…. 'Since each of these membranes has its own darkness when God mentioned the stages of creation and transformation from one state to another, He also mentioned the darkness of the membranes'. Most commentators explain, and here are the words of the commentators… 'It is the darkness of the belly and the darkness of the womb and the darkness of the placenta'. In a second example, we read, Hippocrates said… 'The mouth opens up spontaneously and the nose and ears are formed from the flesh. The ears are opened and the eyes, which are filled with a clear liquid.'

The Prophet used to say… *'I worship Him who made my face and formed it, and opened my hearing, and eyesight and so forth'*. Here we look at Hippocrates again, and they are in the second stage. It is the same thing, which I read. Ibn Khaima is quoting Hippocrates, and speaks about the mother's blood that descends around the membrane.

He could do this as we have seen, because the educated people of Mohammed's time were familiar with Greek medicine. However, what is important for us here today to realise that there is no place where the Qur'an corrected Greek medicine. There is no place for Ibn Khaima shouting…"Hey you guys you got it this all wrong — the correct meaning of '*Alaqa*' is, 'that which clings', or 'leach'-like substance."

On the other hand, even Khaima is demonstrating the agreement between the Qur'an and the Greek medicine. Their agreement is in error. A final witness is the commentary of Badawi in 1200 A.D. Here, we have the commentary. We have the Qur'an here, we have his commentary, and here it is being translated. And then, he says from '*Alaqa*'…'a piece of solid blood', is his explanation of '*Alaqa*'; and '*Alaqa*' is underlined — that is from the Qur'an. And here is his explanation… 'A piece of solid blood.' Then he goes on saying… 'Then from a piece of meat'— from the Qur'an. 'A piece of meat originally as much as can be chewed, and so forth.'

As I mentioned in the beginning of the study, it's been said that the idea of the embryo developing through stages, is a modern one and that the Qur'an is anticipating modern embryology by depicting different stages. Yet, we have seen that Aristotle, Hippocrates, the Indians and Galen — all of who have discussed the stages of embryological development during the thousand years before the Qur'an. And after the coming of the Qur'an, the court of the different stages, as described by the Qur'an and the Greek doctors, was carried on in the teachings of Avisena and Ibn Khaima - and is essentially the same as taught by Galen and those preceding him.

Concerning the bone stage, it is clear as Dr. Moore demonstrated so capably in his text book that muscles start forming from the Semites, at the same time as the cartilage models of the bone. There is no bone stage where there is a skeleton sitting here and then the muscles are plastered around it. It is equally clear that *'Alaqa'* in the Qur'an, means 'clot' — and that the Quraish who heard Mohammed speaking, understood him to be referring to the menstrual blood as the female contribution to the developing baby.

Therefore, we can conclude that during all these years, the Qur'anic Verses on embryology, saying that man is created from a drop of sperm, which becomes the clot, were in perfect record with the science of the 1st century of the Hijra, of the time of the Qur'an. But when compared to the modern science of the 20th century, Hippocrates is in error, Aristotle is in error, Galen is in error, and the Qur'an is in error - They all are in serious error.

Now we are going to look at a little bit about 'moon light.' Does the Qur'an state that... *'The moon gives off reflected light from the sun', before his was common knowledge?* In the Surah Noor, 71: 15 - 16, it says... *'See ye not how Allah has created the seven heavens, one above another and made the moon a light... 'Nur' in their midst, and made the sun as a lamp... 'Siraj.'* The moon is called a 'light'...Arabic *'Nur'* - and

27

the sun a lamp -'*Siraj*'.

Some Muslims claim that since the Qur'an uses different words, speaking from about the light of the sun and the light of the moon, it reveals that the sun is a source of light while the moon only reflects light. This claim is implied very strongly by Shabbir Ali in his booklet... '**Science in the Qur'an**' — and stated clearly by Dr. Zakir Naik in his Video — '**Is the Qur'an God's Word**' as you will now see clearly.

'*Munir*' is a borrowed light while '*Nur*' is a reflection of light In a rejoinder to Dr. Campbell's statements, Dr. Zakir Naik's video clipping on this particular topic was put on in which he is found saying: "The light that we have, is obtained from the moon — where does it come from? So he will tell me that previously we thought that the light of the moon was its own light. But today after science has advanced, we have come to know that the light of the moon is not its own light, but a reflected light of the sun. I will ask him a question, which is mentioned in this Qur'an in Surah Al- Furqaan, Ch. No.25, Verse No.61...'*Blessed is He, who has created the constellation and placed therein a lamp and a moon which has reflected light*'. The Arabic word for moon is '*Qamar*', and the light described there is '*Munir*'—which is borrowed light or 'Nur', which is a 'reflection of light.' The Qur'an mentions that the light of the moon is reflected light. You say you have discovered it today? How come is it mentioned in the Qur'an 1400 years ago? He will pause for a time - He won't reply immediately and then he may say...'May be, may be it is a fluke.' I don't argue with him for this sake..."

Dr. Campbell resumes his speech, saying: Near the end of the

28

video, we heard Dr. Naik explained the Arabic word for 'moon' is '*Qamar*', and the light described there is '*Munir*', which is a 'borrowed light' or '*Nur*', which is a reflection of light.' Please do not forget what he said... '*Munir* is borrowed light, and Nur is reflected light.' Not only is this claim to be a statement in keeping with scientific truth, but it also claimed to be scientifically miraculous since this was supposedly only discovered relatively, recently.

MOON DOES NOT EMIT ITS OWN LIGHT

It is correct that the moon does not emit its own light, but only reflects the light of the sun. But this was known already almost a thousand years before Mohammed. Aristotle in about 360 B.C discussed, knowing that the earth was round, by its shadow on the moon. He could only speak of the earth's shadow crossing the moon, if he knew that the moon's light is reflected light.

If you still insist that this is a miracle of scientific knowledge, then we must ask ourselves... 'Do the Qur'anic words themselves support this claim?' First we shall look at '*Siraj*.' In Surah Nur which was read above, in Surah Al Furqaan, 25:61, it is simply 'lamp'... referring to the sun. In Surah Naba, 78:13, '*Sirajan Wahhjan*' means 'a dazzling lamp', again indicating the sun. The words 'Nur' and '*Munir*' come from the same Arabic word - root. The word Munir is used 6 times in the Qur'an 4 times in Surah Al-Imran, 3:184, Al Haj 22:8, Luqman 31:20 and Fatir 35:35.

It is the phrase '*Kitabul Munir*', which Yusuf Ali translates as... 'A book of enlightenment' and Pickthall uses... 'The Scripture giving light.' Clearly, this indicates a book, which is radiating the light of knowledge. Nothing about 'reflection'... '*Nur*'. It says in

29

Surah Nur, 71:16 and Yunus, 10:5 that... *'Allah made the light... the Moon a light.'* Thus, we find that the Qur'an says that the moon is a light, and it never says that the moon reflects light.

Moreover in other Verses, the Qur'an says that... 'Allah is a Nur... a light.' Surah Nur, 24:35, one of the most beautiful passages in the Qur'an reads... 'Allah is the light... Nur of the Heavens and the Earth. The parable of His light, is as if there was a niche and within it a lamp, the lamp enclosed in glass. The glass as it was a brilliant star and so forth.' Thus, we see that the word 'Nur' is used for both, 'the moon' and 'Allah.'

Are we going to say that Allah gives off reflected light? I think not. But if you continue to insist that 'Nur' used for the moon, means 'borrowed' or 'reflected light', and we saw above that Allah is 'the light'... Nur of the Heavens and the Earth - What is the source of this light? 'Siraj', of which Allah is only a reflection. Think about it. If Allah is named 'Nur' or a 'reflected light'... who or what is the 'Siraj'?

Well! The Qur'an tells us who the 'Siraj' is. But the answer will shock you. In Surah Al Ahzab, 33:45, 46 we find... *'O Prophet! Surely We have send thee as a witness - A bearer of glad tidings and a warner, and as a lamp spreading light'*. Here, it says that Mohammed is the lamp spreading light. In Arabic, it is *'Sirajaam Munira'*. Linguistically and spiritually, this is the end of the discussion. Linguistically *'Siraj'* and the adjective 'Moon' here are used together for the same shining thing — the person Mohammed. It is clear that *'Munir'* does not mean reflected light in this verse – or in any other verse. It means shining.

The people of Mohammed's time understood that the moon was

shining, and they were right. Just as the people of Moses' time understood that the sun was the greater light, and the moon the lesser light and they were right. But if you insist the Arabic words 'Nur' and 'Moon' here mean reflected light, then based on the use of these words in the Qur'an, Mohammed is like the 'Sun' and 'Allah' is like the 'Moon.' Does Dr. Naik really want to say that Mohammed is the source of light, and Allah is only his reflection? Why are these so called scientific claims made, which no Muslim can support, if he makes a serious study of his own Qur'an.

THE FOUR STAGES OF WATER CYCLE

In a dialogue like tonight it makes an honest discussion is very difficult — almost impossible. Let's go on and look at the Water Cycle. Some Muslim authors claim that the Qur'an shows pre-scientific knowledge of Water cycle. What is the water cycle? Here in this slide, you see four steps. **The first step** is evaporation. The water evaporates from the seas and the earth. **Second step** – it becomes clouds. **Third step** – it gives rain. And **fourth** – this rain causes the plants to grow. All these seem all very straightforward, and everybody knows 2, 3 and 4. Even if they live in a town, they know that clouds come and rain comes, and then flowers grow. But what about step one – 'the evaporation.' We cannot see it. It is difficult. And the Qur'an does not have **step one**.

Now we are going to look at a Prophet from the Bible – the Prophet from 700 B.C… Prophet Amos; and he writes: 'He who made the Pleiades and Orion, Who turns blackness into dawn, and darkens day into night, and then Who calls out for the waters, of the sea.'… Stage one —And pours them out over the face of

31

the land… stage three - The Lord (Yahweh) is His name. And one other Prophet is Job, in 36:26-28, at least a thousand years before the Hijra. He says: 'How great is God – beyond our understanding! The number of his years is past finding out'.

Stage one – He draws up the drops of water which distils from the mist as rain that is stage three; and then the clouds are mentioned – Stage two - Which pour down their moisture and abundant showers fall on mankind. So here in the Bible, this difficult stage one is there for more than a thousand years before the Qur'an.

GOD PLACED FIRM AND UNMOVEABLE MOUNTAINS ON THE EARTH.

Now let's go on and look at Mountains. The Qur'an has more than a dozen Verses stating that God placed firm and unmoveable mountains on the Earth. And in some of these Verses, the mountains are listed as either a blessing for believers or a warning for the unbelievers. One example of this is found in the Surah Luqman, 31:10,11, where the mountains are one of five warnings. It says: '*He has created the heavens without support, that you can see, and has cast aalqa onto the earth…'firm mountain'– 'Rawaasiya'*, lest it should shake with you'.

In 'The Prophets'… Al-Ambiya, 21:31, as one of seven warnings we read… '*And We have set on the earth, firm mountains lest it should shake with you… with them.*' Finally in 'The Bee'… Nahl, 16:15, says that… '*He has cast 'alqaa' onto the earth… 'Firm mountains' 'Rawaasiya', lest it should shake with you.* We see then that the believers and the Non-believers are told that Allah has done this great thing - He strolled down and placed the mountains, so that the earth will not shake violently with them'. Therefore, we must ask ourselves… 'What did they understand?'

In the next two Verses, another picture is given, 'The News', Al-Naba 78: 6-7... *"Have We not made the Earth an expanse, and the mountains as stakes 'Al –jebaala awtaad', as those used to anchor a tent in the ground"*. And then 'The Overwhelming' Al-Ghashiya, 88:17-19... 'Do they (the unbelievers) not look at the mountains... 'Al-jibaal'... how they have been pitched like a tent.' Here, men are told that the mountains are placed as tent-pegs, which keep the tents stable. So again, the idea is put forward that the pegs... the mountains will keep the earth from shaking.

THE FORMING OF MOUNTAINS CAUSES EARTHQUAKE

A third picture is presented in the word *'Rawaasiya'*, used for mountains. This word comes from the Arabic root *'Arsa.'* And the same root is used for the Arabic word for 'anchor.' To 'throw out' or 'cast the anchor' is *algaa almirsaa*. So instead of 'Cast the anchor to keep the ship from moving' - *'We have cast the mountains, to keep the earth from shaking'*. From these pictures, it is clear that Mohammed's followers understood that the mountains were thrown down like tent-pegs to keep a tent in place like an anchor to hold the ship in place - to stop the earth from moving or limit earthquakes. But in fact this is false.

The forming of mountains causes earthquake. Therefore, these Verses present a definite problem. Dr. Maurice Bucaille recognised this, and discussed them in his book... **'The Bible, the Qur'an and Science.'** After quoting the above Verses about 'Mountains', he says... 'Modern Geologists described the faults in the earth, as giving foundations to the mountains, and the stability of the earth's crust results from this phenomenon of these faults.

When asked about this, Professor of Geology, Dr. David A. Young says: 'While it is true that many mountain ranges are composed of folded rocks and the folds may be of large scale, it is not true that the folds render the crust stable. The very existence of the fold, is evidence of instability in the crust.' In other words, mountains don't keep the earth from shaking — their formation caused and still causes the surface of the earth to shake.

Geological theories of the present time propose that the hardened crust of the earth is made of sections and plates, which slowly move with relation to each other. Sometimes, the plates separate like North and South America, separating from Europe and South Africa. And sometimes, they go together and they slide next to each other, and they bump into each other, and then they cause earthquakes. An example of this type of mountain formation is found in the Middle East, where the migration of Arabia towards Iran has resulted in the Zygross range in Iran.

In many parts of the world, as one travels along the roads, one sees a hillside where the sandstorm layers which were horizontal at the time of their deposition, are now sticking up at angles. And so here, you can see these sandstorm layers, which were horizontal in the beginning, now they are striking up at 75 degrees. They were pushed up there by an earthquake, by the mountains being formed. Sometimes, the plates get caught on each other and start sliding. During this period, great forces are built up. When the forces of friction are overcome, the piece of plate stuck there, lurches forward, causing a shock wave of a thrust quake, and then all of a sudden it goes 'dumb' like this.

In a recent earthquake, it was calculated that the Coco Splade in

Mexico suddenly jumped forward 3 meters. Well, if your house suddenly jumps 3 meters, there will be a Catastrophe. Another type of mountain is that, which is formed by volcanoes. Lava and ash from inside the earth are thrown out and piled up until a high mountain is formed — Even from the bottom of the sea. And we can see this kind of action in this picture. I hope you can see it — Not clear, is it? The ocean crust is right here and the continental crust is there, and the oceanic crust is going down under the continental crust, and mountains have been found here. Here is the volcano, and here is the magma of the molten rock, going up through the volcano, and here is another volcano with magma going up. And so this is how the mountains are formed and earthquakes are formed.

In the case of some igneous mountains, molten rock intrudes into the probe of the volcano's opening and cools to form a relatively dense intrusion, which extends below the surface of the earth. So if this gets stuck and sealed, then it would be like a plug. However, it is not a root. It does not bear the weight of the mountain. It is really a plug. Therefore, at occasions, pressure builds up under the plug, and the volcano explodes as happened in the South Pacific at Crackato in 1883 when the whole island was blown away. And it happened at Mount Saint Helena in Ardase, when a mountain was blown away.

MOUNTAINS ARE FORMED ORIGINALLY WITH MOVEMENT AND SHAKING

We can conclude from this information that mountains were formed originally with movement and shaking, and that now in the present, earthquakes are caused by their continued formation. When the plates buckle over each other, there are earthquakes.

When the volcanoes erupt there, they can bring earthquake. However, it is clear that the followers of Mohammed were understanding these Verses to say that Allah threw the mountains down as a tent-peg or anchors to keep the Earth from shaking. Throwing the mountains down under the Earth may be poetry, but to say that mountains keep the Earth from shaking, is a severe difficulty, which is out of step with modern science.

Now we are going to take a little look at what the 'Sun' says about... what the Qur'an says about the 'Sun.' In the Surah Kahf, 18:86, it says: *'Until when Zulqarnain (the Alexandar the great) reached the setting of the sun, he found it set in a spring of murky water.'* I'm sorry — In 20th Century Science, the sun does not set in a spring of murky water. And then in 'The Criterion', Al-Furqaan, 25:45 to 46, it says: *'Hast thou not turned thy vision, to thy Lord - how He prolongs the shadow! If He willed, He could make it stationary! Then do We (God) make the sun its guide'.* What about this? If we think of the sun overhead, you have no shadow or a little tiny shadow, and then as the sun goes down, your shadow gets longer on the other side.

THE SUN IS STATIONARY IN RELATION TO THE EARTH

The sun is stationary in relation to the earth; it is not what causes the shadow to shift. The rotating earth guides the shadows. So if you demand 20th century accuracy, the Surah should say... 'The rotating earth causes the shadows to change. I would look at a different subject... 'Solomon's death.' Whether this is Science, I don't know - May be Sociology. Solomon's death – He is popped up on his staff. Says... *'The jinn worked for him, as Solomon desired. 'Then when We decreed death upon*

Solomon, nothing showed them his death, except a little creeping creature of the earth, which gnawed away his staff. And when he fell, the jinn saw clearly'. If they had known the unseen, they would not have continued in the humiliating penalty of work. So here Solomon is dead, propped up on his staff like a walker from Morocco overseeing only a road gay, and no cook comes to ask him as to what he wants for dinner. And no General comes for orders, and none of his Nobles comes to say... 'Let's go for hunting.' No one notices. I'm sorry — I do not believe this story and it won't fit 20th century Sociology or 7th century Sociology, where the king will never be left alone like that.

Now finally let's look at 'Milk.' It says in the Surah of 'The Bee', Nahl, 16:66... *'We pour out to you from what is within their (the cattle's) abdomen, between excretions and blood – milk, pure and agreeable to the drinkers.'* The abdomen where the intestines are. In 20th century medical science, the abdomens where the intestines are, is the mammary glands are under the skin. In humans, they are under the skin. In cattle, they are under the skin between the legs. There is no connection between the breasts and the intestines, and the their faeces, in any way. Faeces though in the body, it really is outside of the animal. Animals have finished with it. It is not connected to milk or to anything else.

And finally going to look at 'Communities.' The Surah of 'The Cattle', Al – Anam 6:38, *'There is not an animal on the earth, nor a being that flies on two wings, but forms communities like you...'.* Speaks about no animal on earth, not a being that flies, and then it says that every one of them is communities like you. And I assume that the Qur'an is speaking about us—the humans.

In some spiders, when they finishes mating, the mother eats the father. I'm glad that my wife did not eat me. Even in bees, the extra male Drones are thrown out to die. I'm glad also that after we had four children, my wife did not push me out of the house too.

Finally, when the male lion gets old, a young lion comes along and drives him away from his own wife, and then the young lion takes over the wives. But what he does with the cubs of the old lion? He kills them all. So I do not think that this stance is true that all other communities and all other animals do not live as communities like us.

In conclusion, it is clear that the Qur'an has many scientific errors. As a generality, the Qur'an meets and reflects the science of its time - the science of the 7th century AD. We have come here to seek truth, and I've done my best to present valid information. If you want to see all the references, my book, **'The Qur'an and the Bible:In the light of History and Science'** is for sale at a bargain price, tonight. May the God of all truth, guide you. Thank you.

Dr. Mohammed thanks Dr. Campbell for his presentation, and then requests Dr. Sabeel Ahmed to introduce the next speaker, Dr. Zakir Naik to speak on the concerned topic. On Dr. Mohammed's invitation to speak on the concerned topic, Zakir Naik starts his speech with Islamic greetings and saying thanks to all with the words as thus:

Respected Dr. William Campbell, Dr. Maracuss, Dr. Jamal Badavi, Br. Samuel Nauman, Dr. Mohammed Naik, my respected elders and my dear brothers and sisters, I welcome all of you with the Islamic greetings... 'Assalaam-u- Alaikum Wa Rahmatullahi

Wa Barkatahu—May peace mercy and blessings of Allah *Subhanahu-wa-taala* be on all of you. The topic of today's dialogue is 'The Qur'an and the Bible in the light of Science.'

THE QUR'AN IS THE MIRACLE OF MIRACLES

The Glorious Qur'an is the last and final Revelation which was revealed to the last and final Messenger Prophet Mohammed, Peace be upon him. For any book to claim that it is a Revelation from Almighty God, it should stand the test of time. Previously in the olden days, it was the age of miracles - *Alhamdulillah*, the Qur'an is the miracle of miracles. Later on, came the age of literature and poetry, and Muslims and Non-Muslims alike claim the Glorious Qur'an to be the best Arabic literature available on the face of the Earth. But today is the age of Science and Technology.

MORE THAN A THOUSAND AYATS IN THE QUR'AN SPEAK ABOUT SCIENCE

Let's analyse whether the Qur'an is compatible or incompatible with modern science. Albert Einstein said, 'Science without Religion is lame, and Religion without Science is blind'. Let me remind you that the Glorious Qur'an is not a book of Science...S-C-I-E-N-C-E, It is a book of signs S-I-G-N-S... It is a book of Ayats. And there are more than 6000 signs... *Ayats* in the Glorious Qur'an out of which more than a thousand speak about science. As far as my talk regarding the Qur'an and Science is concerned, I will only be speaking about scientific facts which have been established. I will not be speaking about the scientific hypothesis and the theories, which are based on assumption without any proof, because we all know many a times science takes U-turns.

Dr. William Campbell who wrote a reply to the book of Dr. Maurice

Bucaille… 'The Qur'an and the Bible:In the light of History and Science', says in his book that there are two types of approaches. One is a concordance approach, which means a person tries to bring compatibility between the Scripture and Science. And the other is the conflict approach, in which a person tries to bring a conflict between Scripture and Science, like how Dr. William Campbell has done very well. But as far as the Qur'an is concerned, irrespective of whether a person uses a conflict approach or a concordance approach – As long as you are logical, and after a logical explanation is given to you, not a single person will be able to prove a single Verse of the Qur'an in conflict with established modern science.

Dr. William Campbell has pointed out various alleged scientific errors in the Qur'an, and I am supposed to actually refute in the rebuttal. But since he chose to speak first, I will be refuting a few points in my talk. I will reply to the major part of his talk, mainly dealing with Embryology and with Geology. The remaining *Insha-Allah* I will try my level best to reply in the rebuttal. I have to do both — I cannot do injustice to the topic. The topic is… 'The Qur'an and the Bible in the light of Science.' I cannot speak about only one Scripture. Dr. William Campbell hardly spoke about one or two points about the Bible, which I will deal with *Insha-Allah*. I will speak about both, as I want to do justice to the topic.

As far as the Qur'an and modern Science is concerned, in the field of 'Astronomy', the Scientists and the Astronomers, a few decades earlier, described as to how the universe came into existence. They call it the 'Big Bang'. And they said… 'Initially there was one primary nebula, which later on separated it with a Big Bang, which gave rise to Galaxies, Stars, Sun and the Earth, we live in.' This information is given in a nutshell in the Glorious Qur'an in Surah Ambiya, Ch. 21, Verse No. 30, which says: '*Do not the unbelievers see? That the heavens and the earth were joined together, and we clove them asunder.*' Imagine this information which we came to know recently, the Qur'an mentions 14 hundred years ago.

MODERN SCIENCE HAS CONFIRMED THE QUR'ANIC STATEMENT

When I was in school, I had learned that the Sun in respect to the earth was stationary. The earth and the moon rotated about in axis, but the Sun was stationary. But when I read a Verse of the Qur'an, saying in Surah Al–Ambiya, Ch. 21 Verse No. 33, it says: '*It is Allah who has created the night and the day; the sun and the moon. Each one travelling in an orbit with its own motion*'. Now *Alhamdulillah*, modern Science has confirmed the Qur'anic statement.

THE QUR'AN SAYS THAT THE SUN AND THE MOON ROTATE AROUND THEIR OWN AXIS

The Arabic word used in the Qur'an is '*Yasbahoon*', which describes the motion of a moving body. When it refers to a celestial body, it means it is rotating about its own axis. So, the Qur'an says that the Sun and the Moon revolve as well as rotate about their own axis. Today, we have come to know that the Sun takes approximately 25 days to complete one rotation. It was Edvin Hubbel who discovered that the Universe is expanding.

The Qur'an says in Surah *Dhariyat*, Ch. 51, Verse No. 47, that…'*We have created the expanding universe*' - *The vastness of space.* The Arabic word '*Mohsiana*' refers to 'vastness' – 'the expanding Universe.' Regarding the topics on

41

Astronomy, which Dr. William Campbell touched, I will deal in the rebuttal, *Insha-Allah.*

In the field of 'Water Cycle, Dr. William Campbell pointed out certain things. The Qur'an describes the Water Cycle in great detail. And Dr. Campbell mentioned 4 stages. In his book he mentions 4 (a) and (b) — the last one he did not mention in the slide — I don't know why? It says... 'The Driplinition'—'The Water table.' He missed out here — Maybe because it was not mentioned in the Bible. He said there is not a single Verse in the Qur'an, which speaks about 'Evaporation.'

The Qur'an says in Surah Al-Tariq, Ch. No. 86, Verse No. 11, that... *'By the capacity of the heavens to return.'* And almost all the commentaries of the Qur'an — they said that this Verse of Surah Tariq, Ch. No. 86, Verse No. 11, refers to the capacity of the heavens to return back rain, meaning 'Evaporation.' Dr. Campbell, who knows Arabic, may say... 'Why did not Allah *Subhanahu-wa-Taala* specifically mention the meaning... 'The capacity of the heavens to return back rain?'

Now we have come to know why did not Allah do that in His Divine wisdom. Because, today we have come to know that besides — the Ozonosphere—the layer above the earth — Besides returning back rain, it even returns back other beneficial matter and energy of the earth, which is required by the human beings. It does not only return back rain, but today, we have also come to know that it even returns back waves of Telecommunication, of Television, of Radio, by which we can see TV, we can communicate, we can hear the radio. And besides that, it even returns back the harmful rays of the outer space, back on the other side, and absorbs. For example, the ultraviolet

42

rays of the sunlight are absorbed by the Ionosphere. If this were not done, life on the earth would have ceased to exist. So Allah *Subhanahu-wa-Taala* is far superior and more accurate, when He says, '**By the capacity of the Heaven to return.**' And the remaining things as he mentioned is there in the Qur'an — You can refer to my Video-cassette.

The Qur'an describes the 'Water Cycle' in great detail; regarding what he said about the Bible, he showed stage 1 and stage 3 in the first slide, and in the second stage 1, 3, and then 2. 'That the rain water is taken up'... he says... 'And then the rain water comes down on the Earth.' This is the philosophy of Phasofmillitas, in 7th century B.C. He thought that the spray of the ocean was picked up by the wind, and sent to the interior as rain. There is no cloud mentioned there.

THE QUR'AN DESCRIBES THE WATER CYCLE IN GREAT DETAIL

In the second quotation, Dr. William Campbell gave — First is, according to him, 'Evaporation' which we agree. We don't mind having the concordance approach with the Bible. '...Then rain falls down, and then are the clouds formed.' - That is not the complete Water Cycle. *Alhamdulillah*, the Qur'an describes the Water Cycle in great detail in several places. How does the water rise, evaporates, forms into clouds - the clouds join together, they stalk up, there is thunder and lightning, water comes down, the clouds move into the interior, they fall down as rain, and the evaporation of the water table and so on.

The Qur'an speaks about the Water Cycle in at several places in Surah Nur, Ch. No. 24, Verse No. 43, in Surah Rum, Ch. No. 30, Verse 48, in Surah Al-Zumar, Ch. 39, Verse 21, in Surah

Muminun, Ch. 23, Verse 18, in Surah Rum Ch. No. 30, Verse No. 24, in Surah Al-Hijr, Ch. 15, Verse No. 22, in Surah A'raf Ch. No. 7, Verse No. 57, in Surah Rad, Ch. No. 13, Verse No. 17, in Surah Furqan, Ch. 25, Verse No. 48 and 49, in Surah Fatir, Ch. No. 35, Verse No. 9, in Surah Yasin, Ch. 36, Verse No. 34, in Surah Jathiya, Ch. 45, Verse No. 5, in Surah Qaf, Ch. No. 50, Verse No. 9, in Surah Al-Waqiah, Ch. No. 56, Verse No. 68 and 70, in several places, Surah Al-Mulk,Ch. 67, Verse No. 30, the Glorious Qur'an speaks about the 'Water Cycle' in great detail.

Dr. William Campbell spent maximum time, about half of his talk on 'Embryology', quite a lot on Geology and touched on other six topics, which I've noted down. In the field of Geology, we have come to know today about the Geologists, who tell us that the radius of the earth is approximately 3750 miles, and the deeper layers are hot and fluid, and cannot sustain life. And the superficial part of the Earth's crust, which we live on, is very thin - hardly 1 to 30 miles. Some portions are thicker, but the majority is of one to 30 miles. And there are high possibility that this superficial layer, the earth's crust will shake. It is due to the 'Folding phenomenon', which gives rise to mountain ranges, which gives stability to this earth.

THE QUR'AN DOES NOT SAY THAT THE MOUNTAINS WERE THROWN UP AS STAKES

The Qur'an says in Surah Nabaa, Ch. No. 78, Verse No. 6 and 7…'*We have made the Earth as an expanse and the mountains as stakes.*' The Qur'an does not say mountains were thrown up as stakes. Arabic word '*Autaad*' means 'stakes'… meaning 'tent-peg'. And today we have come to know in the

44

study of modern Geology that mountain has got deep roots. This was known in the second half of the 19th century. And the superficial part that we see of the mountain, is a very small percentage. The deeper part is within — Exactly like a stake how it is driven in the ground.

You can only see a small part on the top, and the majority is down in the ground or like a tip of the iceberg. You can see the tip on the top and about 90% are beneath water. The Qur'an says in Surah Ghashiya, Ch. 88, Verse No. 19, and Surah Naziat, Ch. No. 79, Verse No. 32: '*And We have made the mountains standing firm on the Earth*'.

Today, after modern Geology has advanced, and Dr. William Campbell said that... 'By the theory of Platectonics — It was propounded in 1960, which gives rise to mountain ranges.' The Geologists today, do say that the mountains give stability to the Earth — Not all Geologists, but many do say. I have not come across a single geological book, and I challenge Dr. William Campbell to produce a single geological book - Not his personal correspondence with the Geologist. That does not carry weight. His personal correspondence with Dr. Keith Moore... Documented proof. And if you read the book, '**The Earth**' which is referred by almost all the universities in the field of Geology, one of its authors by the name of Dr. Frank Press, who was the advisor to the former president of USA, Jimmy Carter, and was the president of the Academy of Science of USA, writes in his book that... 'The mountains are wedge shaped - It has deep roots within'. And he says that... 'The function of the mountain is to stabilise the earth.' And the Qur'an says in Surah Ambiya, Ch. No 21, Verse No. 31, in Surah Luqman, Ch. No. 31 Verse No.10, as well as in

Surah Nahl, Ch. No. 16, Verse No. 15, that…'*We have made the mountains standing firm on the Earth, lest it would shake with them and with you.*'

NOWHERE DOES THE QUR'AN SAY THAT MOUNTAINS PREVENT EARTHQUAKE

The function of the mountain in the Qur'an is given to prevent the earth from shaking. Nowhere does the Qur'an say that the mountain prevents the earthquake. And Dr. William Campbell said - He writes in his book, and even the talk, that… 'You find in the mountain regions, there are various earthquakes, and mountains cause earthquake.' The point to be noted is that nowhere does the Qur'an say that mountains prevent earthquake.

The Arabic word for 'earthquake' as Dr. William Campbell knows Arabic, is '*zilzaal*' or '*zalzala*' but the words used in these three Verses I quoted, is '*Tamida.*'which means 'to shake', 'to 'sway', 'to swing.' And the Qur'an says in Surah Luqman, Ch. 31, Verse No. 10, as well as Surah Nahl, Ch. No. 16 Verse No. 15…'*We have put on the earth mountains standing firm, lest it would shake with you*'. It is '*tamide bikum*'…'Shake with you', Indicating, if the mountains were not there, if you would have walked, if you would have moved, even the earth would have moved with you —If you would have swayed, even the earth would have swayed with you. And we know normally when we walk on the earth, it does not shake, and the reason for this is, according to Dr. Frank Press and Dr. Najjat who is from Saudi Arabia, and he wrote a full book on the Geological concepts in the Qur'an, answering almost everything in detail what Dr. William

Campbell has said. And Dr. William Campbell in his book writes that…'If mountains prevent the shaking of the earth, then how come you find earthquakes in the mountains regions.'
I said, nowhere does the Qur'an say, mountains prevent earthquake. Earthquake is '*zilzaal*', and if you see the definition in the Oxford dictionary, it says… Earthquake is due to convulsion of the superficial crust of the Earth, due to relief of compressed seismic waves, due to crack in the rock, or due to volcanic reaction. The Qur'an speaks about '*zalzala*' in Surah *Zilzaal*, Ch. 99. But here, it speaks about '*Tamida bikum*'- 'to prevent the earth from shaking with you.' And in reply to the statement…'That if mountains prevent earthquakes, how come you find earthquakes in mountainous regions?' The reply is, that if I say that medical doctors prevent the sickness and diseases in a human being, and if someone argues, if doctors prevent the sickness and diseases in a human being, how come you find more sick people in the hospitals, where there are more doctors than at home —where there are no doctor.'
In the field of Oceanology, the Glorious Qur'an says, in Surah Furqan, Ch. No. 25, Verse No. 53, that…'*It is Allah who has let free two bodies of following water - One sweet and palatable, the other salt and bitter. Though they meet, they do not mix. Between them there is a barrier, which is forbidden to be trespassed*'. The Qur'an says in Surah Rahman, Ch. 55 Verse No. 19 and 20…'*It is Allah who has let free two bodies of flowing water. Though they meet, they do not mix. Between them there is barrier, which is forbidden to be trespassed.*'
THE QUR'AN MENTIONING THE '*BARZAKH*'—

47

UNSEEN BARRIER HAS BEEN AGREED UPON BY SEVERAL SCIENTISTS

Previously, the commentators of the Qur'an wondered... 'What does the Qur'an mean? We know about sweet and salt water, but between them, there is a barrier - though they meet and do not mix. Today after advancement of Oceanology, we have come to know that whenever one type of water flows into the other type of water, it looses its constituents and gets homogenised into the water it flows. There is a slanting homogenising area, which the Qur'an refers to as '*Barzakh*' 'unseen barrier' And this has been agreed upon by several Scientists, even of America, by the name of Dr. Hay who is an Oceanologist.

And Dr. William Campbell writes in his book that... 'It is an observable phenomena. The fisherman of that time knew there were two types of water... salt and sweet. So Prophet Mohammed (S.A.W.) during an expedition to Syria, may have gone in the sea or he might have spoken to those fishermen.' Sweet and salt water is an observable phenomenon, I agree, but people did not know that there was an unseen barrier, until recently. The Scientific point to be noted here is the 'Barzakh' does not indicate the sweet and the salt water.

In the field of Embryology, Dr. William Campbell spent approximately half of his talk on that. Time will not permit me to reply to every small thing, which is illogical. I'll just give a brief reply, which will be satisfactory *Insha-Allah*. And for more details, you can refer to my Video cassette – **'The Qur'an and Modern Science'** and my other cassettes on... **'The Qur'an and Medical Science.'**

ACCORDING TO PROF. KEITH MOORE, MOST OF

THE QUR'ANIC VERSES AND THE HADITH ARE IN PERFECT CONFORMITY WITH MODERN EMBRYOLOGY

There were a group of Arabs who collected the data dealing in the Qur'an about 'Embryology' and the Hadith dealing with Embryology. And they presented it to Professor Keith Moore, who was the Chairman & the Head of the Department of 'Anatomy' in the University of Toronto in Canada. At present, he is one of the leading scientists in the field of 'Embryology.' After reading the various translations of the Qur'an, he was asked to comment, and he said... 'Most of the Verses of the Qur'an and the Hadith are in perfect conformity with Modern Embryology. But there are a few verses, which I cannot say that they are right; neither can I say that they are wrong, because I myself don't know about it. And two such Verses were the first two Verses of the Qur'an to be revealed from Surah Iqra or Surah Alaq, Ch. 96 Verses No. 1 and 2 which says: *'Read, recite or proclaim in the name of thy Lord, Who created the human beings from something which clings - a leech like substance'*.

Regarding Dr. William Campbell's statement that... 'To analyse the meaning of a word, we have to see what was the meaning at that time when it was revealed' or at the time when the book was written. And he rightly said that to analyse the meaning, we have to analyse the meaning at the time it was revealed, and to the people whom it was meant for. As far as this statement of his is concerned, regarding the Bible, I do agree with it totally, because the Bible was only meant for the children of Israel, for that time.

49

UNLIKE THE BIBLE, THE QUR'AN IS MEANT FOR THE WHOLE OF HUMANITY AND ETERNITY.

It is mentioned in the Gospel of Mathew, Ch. No. 10, Verse No. 5 and 6, Jesus Christ (Peace be upon) him tells his disciples… 'Go ye not in the way of the Gentiles.' Who are the Gentiles? The Non-Jews, the Hindus, the Muslims 'But rather go to the lost sheep of the house of Israel.' Jesus Christ (Peace be upon him) said in the Gospel of Mathew, Ch. No. 15, Verse No. 24… 'I am not sent, but to the lost sheep of the house of Israel.' So Jesus Christ and the Bible were only meant for the children of Israel. Since it was meant for them to analyse the Bible, you have to use the meaning of the word, which was utilised at that time. But the Qur'an was not meant only for the Arabs of that time or only for the Muslims. The Qur'an is meant for the whole of humanity, and it is meant to be for eternity.

UNLIKE OTHER PROPHETS, PROPHET MUHAMMAD (S.A.W.) WAS SENT AS A MERCY UPON THE WHOLE HUMANKIND

The Qur'an says in Surah Ibrahim, Ch. 14, Verse. 52 in Surah Baqarah Ch. No. 2, Verse 185, and Surah Zumar Ch. 39, Verses. 41, that the Qur'an is meant for the whole of humankind. And Prophet Mohammed, (May peace be upon him), was not sent only for the Muslims or the Arabs. Allah says in the Qur'an in Surah Ambiya Ch. No. 21, Verse No. 107 That… *'We have sent thee as a mercy, as a guidance, to the whole of humankind.'*

So, as far as the Qur'an is concerned, you cannot limit the meaning only for that time, because it is meant for eternity. So one of the meaning of 'Alaqa'… is 'leech—like substance' or 'something which clings.' So Professor Keith Moore said... 'I did not know whether the early stage of the embryo looks like a leech' And he went into his laboratory, and he analysed the early stage of an embryo under a microscope and compared it with the photograph of a leech, and he was astonished at the striking resemblance. This is a photograph of a leech, and human embryo. What Dr. William Campbell showed you is the other perspective of it. If I show this book, it looks like a rectangle. If I show you like that, it is in a different perspective. That diagram is given in the book which you saw on the slide is even there, and I'll deal with it *Insha-Allah.*

After 80 questions were asked to Professor Keith Moore, he said... 'If you would have asked me these 80 questions 30 years ago, I would not be able to answer more than 50 percent, because embryology has developed recently in the past 30 years.' He said this in the eighties. Now, do we believe Dr. Keith Moore whose statement is available outside in the foyer - his video cassette is available... 'This is the truth'... '*Anna-ul-Haq*'... recorded statement.

So will you believe Dr. William Campbell's personal conversation with Professor Keith Moore or the one mentioned in this book with Islamic edition as well as the photograph that I had shown to you? And in the videocassette available outside you can see it— He makes those statements. So you have to choose which is more logical—Personal discussion with Dr. William Campbell or his statement on Video. Like how Dr. William Campbell showed my video —100 percent proof what I said... 'Moon is reflected light' — I'll come to it later on. And whatever additional information he got from the Qur'an and the Hadith was incorporated later into this book… 'The Developing Human' - the 3rd edition and this book got an award for the best medical book written by a single author in that year. This is the Islamic edition that was put forward by Shaikh Abdul Majeed Al-Jindani and certified by Keith Moore himself.

THE QUR'AN SAYS THAT THE HUMAN BEINGS HAVE BEEN MADE FROM A 'NUTFAA'— MINUTE QUANTITY OF LIQUID

The Qur'an says in Surah Muminun, Ch. 23 Verse No. 13, and Surah Haj Ch. 22, Verse No. 5, and no less than 11 different places in the Qur'an that the human beings have been made from a 'Nutfaa' 'minute quantity of liquid'…like a trickle that is remaining in the cup. 'Nutfa' in Arabic means a very small quantity. Today, we have come to know, that in one seminal emission, in which there are several millions of sperms, only one is required to fertilise the ovum. The Qur'an refers as 'Nutfaa' and says in Surah Sajda Ch. 32 Verse No. 8…'*We have created the human beings from 'Sulalah'*—That means the best part of a whole. The one sperm which fertilises the ova out of the millions of sperms, the Qur'an refers to as 'Sulalah'…'best part of the whole', and it says in Surah Insan, Ch. 76 Verse No. 2…'We have created the human beings from 'nutfatin amshaj' — 'a minute quantity of mingled fluid'— referring to the sperm as well as the ovum — Both are required for the fertilisation.

The Qur'an describes various embryological stages in great detail, of which the slides were shown to you. Dr. William Campbell has helped me to complete this topic. It is mentioned in Surah Muminun Ch. 23, Verses No. 12 to 14 — The translation is that…'*We have created the human beings from a 'Nutfa' (A minute quantity of liquid)'*. Then placed it in 'qaraarim-makiin' (a place of security). Then We made it into an '*Alaqa*' (a leech-like substance — something which clings — a congealed clot of blood). Then We made that 'Alaqa' into a 'Mudgha' (a chewed like-lump). Then We made the 'Mutgha' into '*Izama*' (bones). Then clothed the bones with '*laham*' (flesh). Then We made it a new creature'. Blessed be Allah Who is the best to create.

These 3 Verses of the Qur'an speak about the various embryological stages in great detail. First, the *Nutfa* placed in a place of security - Made into an '*Alaqa*', and *Alaqa* has got 3 meanings - One is 'something' which clings', and we know that in the initial stages, the embryo clings to the uterine wall and continues clinging till the end. Point No.2 that it also means a leech-like substance, and as I discussed earlier, the embryo in the initial stages does look like a leech. Besides looking like a leech, it also behaves like a leech. It receives its blood supply from the mother like a bloodsucker. And the 3rd meaning which Dr. William Campbell objected to — that is the right meaning… 'The congealed clot of blood'. And that is why according to him, the Qur'an has a scientific error.

I do agree with him that Dr. William Campbell did not agree. He said how can it mean a congealed clot of blood, because if this is the case, then the Qur'an is wrong. I am sorry to say that the Qur'an is not wrong. I'll say with due respect to Dr. William that he is wrong, because today after advancement of embryology, even Dr. Keith Moore says that… 'In the initial stages, the embryo, besides looking like a leech, also looks like a congealed clot of blood, because in the initial stages, of the stage of '*Alaqa*', 3 to 4 weeks, the blood is clotted within closed vessels'. And Dr. William Campbell made it easy for me — He showed you a slide. It will
53

be difficult for you to see — But this is the slide he showed you. This is exactly what Professor Keith Moore said... 'Looks like a clot, in which the blood is clotted within closed vessels. And during the 3rd week of the embryo, the blood circulation does not take place — it starts later on. Therefore, it assumes the appearance of a clot. And if you observe the conspectus — that is after abortion takes place, you can see, it looks like a clot. Only one line answer is sufficient to answer all the allegations of Dr. William Campbell that the stages of the Qur'an while it describes the embryological stages, are based only on appearance.

First is the appearance of the '*Alaqa*', a 'leech-like substance' as well as a clot of blood.' And Dr. William Campbell rightly said that some ladies come and ask... 'Please remove the clot' — It does look like a clot. And the stages are based on appearance. It is created from something, which appears like a clot, which appears like a leech, and is also something which clings. Then the Qur'an says... 'We made the '*Alaqa*' into '*Mudga*' – a chewed like-lump.'

THE STAGES OF EMBRYO ARE DIVIDED ON APPEARANCE, NOT ON THE FUNCTION

Professor Keith Moore took plastic seal, and bit between his teeth to make it look-like a '*Mudgha*'—The teeth marks resembled the 'somites.' Dr. William Campbell said... 'When the '*Alaqa*' becomes a '*Mudgha*' the clinging is yet there —It is there till 8 and a half months. So, the Qur'an is wrong.' I told you in the beginning, the Qur'an is describing the appearance. 'The leech-like' appearance or the 'clot-like' appearance is changed to the 'chewed'-like appearance. It yet continues to cling till the end; there is no problem; but the stages are divided on appearance — Not on the function.

54

Later on, the Qur'an says... 'We made the '*Mudgha*' into '*Izama*'...bones —Then clothed the bones with flesh.' Dr. William Campbell said, and I do agree with him, that... 'The precursors of the muscles and the cartilagees... that is the bones, they form together'. Today, embryology tells us that the primordial of the muscles and the bones form together between the 25th and the 40th day, which the Qur'an refers to as the stage of '*Mudgha*' but they are not developed.

Later on, at the end of the seventh week, the embryo takes form of human appearance, and then the bones are formed. Today, modern embryology says that the bones are formed after the 42nd day, and it gives an appearance of a skeletal thing. Even at this stage when the bones are formed, the muscles are not formed. Later on, after the 7th week and the starting of 8th week, the muscles are formed. Thus, the Qur'an is perfect in describing first '*Alaqa*', then '*Mudgha*', then '*Izama*', then clothed with flesh, and when they form — the description is perfect.

As Professor Keith Moore said that... 'The stages — that how it is described in modern embryology... stage 1,2,3,4,5, is so confusing. The Qur'anic stage on embryology describing on the base of appearance and the shape is far more superior.' Therefore, he said that... 'I have no objection in accepting that Prophet Muhammed is the Messenger of God and that this Glorious Qur'an has to be a Divine Revelation from Almighty God.'

It is mentioned in Surah Nisa, Ch. No. 4, Verse No. 56, which speaks about 'Pain.' Previously, the doctors thought that the brain was only responsible for feeling of 'pain.' Today, we have come to know besides the brain, there are certain receptors in the skin, which are responsible for feeling of the pain, which we call as the 'pain receptors.' Allah say in the Qur'an in Surah Nisa Ch. 4, Verse 56, that... *As to those who reject Our signs, We shall cast them into the hellfire, and as often as their skins are roasted, We shall give them fresh skin, so that they shall feel the pain'*. It indicates that there is something in the skin, which is responsible for feeling of pain, which the Qur'an refers to as **'pain receptors.**

Professor Thagada Shaun, who is the Head of the Department of Anatomy in Chang Mai University in Thailand, — Only on the basis of this one Verse, proclaimed the *Shahada* in the 8th Medical conference in Riyadh. He said; 'There is no God but Allah, and Prophet Mohammed, (Peace be upon him), is the Messenger of Allah'. I started my talk by quoting the Verse from the Glorious Qur'an from Surah Fussilat, Ch. 41, Verse 53, which says... 'That soon We shall show them Our signs in the farthest reaches of the horizons, and into their souls, until it is clear to them, that this is the truth.' This one Verse was sufficient to prove to Dr. Thagada Shaun that the Qur'an is a Divine Revelation. Some may require 10 signs and some 100. Some, even after a 1000 signs are given, they will not accept the truth. The Qur'an calls such people, as in Surah Baqarah Ch. 2, Verse 18... *'The deaf, the dumb, the blind, they will not return to the true path.'*

The Bible says the same thing in Gospel of Mathew, Ch. No. 13, Verse No. 13... 'Seeing they see not, hearing they hear not, neither will they understand.' And regarding the other parts of 'Embryology', I will deal in my rebuttal *Insha-Allah*, if time permits. I have to do justice to the other part also... regarding **The Bible : In the light of science.'**

At the outset, let me tell you, that the Qur'an says in Surah Rad,

Ch. 13, Verse. 38, that... *'We have given several Revelations.'* *By name, only 4 are mentioned - The Torah, the Zaboor, the Injeel and the Qur'an. The Torah is the 'Wahi' the 'Revelation',* which was given to Prophet Moses, (Peace be upon him). The **Zaboor** is the 'Wahi', which was given to David, (Peace be upon him). The Injeel is the 'Wahi', the 'Revelation' which was given to Jesus, (Peace be upon him). And the Qur'an is the last and final Revelation, which was given to the last and final Messenger Prophet Mohammed, (Peace be upon him).

THE BIBLE WHICH THE CHRISTIANS BELIEVE TO BE THE GOD'S WORD, IS NOT THE *'INJEEL'* WHICH THE MUSLIMS BELIEVE

Let me make it very clear to every one that this Bible which the Christians believe to be the word of God, is not the *'Injeel'* which we — the Muslims believe. It was revealed to Prophet Jesus, Peace be upon him. This Bible, according to us, may contain the words of God, but it also contains the words of Prophets, the words of historians, it contains absurdities, obscenity and innumerable scientific errors.

If there are the scientific points mentioned in the Bible, there are possibilities of that — why not? It may be part of the word of God in the Bible, but what about the scientific errors? What about the unscientific portions? Can you attribute this to God? I want to make it very clear to my Christian brothers and sisters —The purpose of my presentation on 'The Bible and science' is not to hurt the feeling of any Christian. While presenting, if I hurt your feelings, I do apologise in advance. The purpose is only to point out that a God's Revelation cannot contain scientific errors. As Jesus Christ, (Peace be upon him) said... 'Search ye the truth,

57

and the truth shall free you.'

We have the Old Testament as well as the New Testament. Now you should follow the Last and Final Testament, which is the Glorious Qur'an. As far as Dr. William Campbell is concerned, I can be more liberal with him, because he has written a book '**The Qur'an and the Bible : In the light of history and science.**' He has given a presentation, and he is a medical doctor - I don't have to be very formal with him. As far as the other Christian brothers and sisters are concerned, I apologise if I hurt your feelings during the presentation.

Let's analyse what the Bible says about modern science. First, we deal with Astronomy. The Bible speaks about the creation of the universe. In the beginning, 1st Book, the Book of Genesis, 1st Ch., it says that the Almighty God created the Heavens and the Earth in six days and talks about an evening and a morning, referring to a 24 - hour day. Today scientists tell us that the universe cannot be created in a 24-hour period of six days. The Qur'an too speaks about six '*ayyams*'. The Arabic word singular is 'yaum' plural is '*ayyam*'. It can either mean a day of 24 hours or it is a very long period, a '*yaum*' — an epoch.

Scientists say we have no objection in agreeing that the universe could have been created in 6 very long periods. Point No.2 – the Bible says in Genesis Ch. No. 1 Verses No. 3 and 5, 'Light was created on the first day.' Genesis, Ch., 1 Verses, 14 to 19… 'The cause of light — stars and the sun, etc. was created on the fourth day'. How can the cause of light be created on the 4th day — latter than the light, which came into existence on the first day? It is unscientific.

Further, the Bible says in Genesis, Ch. 1, Verses 9 to 13… 'Earth

58

was created on the 3rd day'. How can you have a night and day without the earth? The day depends upon the rotation of the Earth. Without the earth created, how can you have a night and day? Point No.4, Genesis, Ch. No. 1 Verses 9 to 13 says… 'Earth was created on the third day.' Genesis Ch. No. 1 Verses 14 to 19 says…'The Sun and the Moon were created on the fourth day.'

Today science tells us… 'Earth is a part of the parent body— the sun.' It cannot come into existence before the sun – It is unscientific. Point No. 5, the Bible says in Genesis, Ch. No.1, Verse No. 11 to 13…'The vegetation, the herbs, the shrubs, the trees were created on the 3rd day'. And the Sun, Genesis, Ch. No. 1, Verses. 14 to 19 say, was created on the 4th day. How can the vegetation come into existence without sunlight, and how can they survive without sunlight? Point No.6, that the Bible says in Genesis, Ch. 1, Verses No.16, that…'God created two lights the greater light, the Sun to rule the day, and the lesser light the Moon, to rule the night'. The actual translation, if you go to the Hebrew text, it is 'lamps'—'Lamps having lights of its own.' And that you will come to know better if you read both the Verses – Genesis, Ch. No.1, Verse. 16, as well as 17. Verse No.17, which says…'And Almighty God placed them in the firmament, to give light to the earth', indicating that the sun and the moon have their own light, which is in contradiction with established scientific knowledge that we have.

There are certain people who try and reconciliate, and say that the six days mentioned in the Bible actually refers to epochs — like the Qur'an refers to long periods — not six, 24 hour day. It is illogical—you read in the Bible, evening and morning. It clearly states 24 hours, which it indicates. But even if I use the concordance approach no problem. I agree with your illogical argument, yet they will only be able to solve the 1st scientific error of 6 days creation, and second, of first day 'light' and 3rd day 'earth.' They cannot solve the remaining four.

Some further say that… 'If it is a 24-hour period, why cannot the vegetables survive for one 24 hour day without sunlight?' I say 'Fine — If you say that the vegetables were created before the sun and can survive for one 24-hour day, I have got no objection. But you cannot say that the days mentioned are 24 hours as well as epochs. You cannot have the cake and eat it, both. If you say it is long period, you solve Point No.1 and 3, the remaining 4 are yet there. If you say that the days are 24 hours day, you solve only Point No.5 — the remaining 5 are yet there - It becomes unscientific. I leave it to Dr. William Campbell, whether he wants to say… 'It is long period', and say that there are only 4 scientific errors or say… 'It is a 24 hour day', and say there is only 5 scientific errors in the creation of the universe.

Regarding the concept of Earth, there are the various scientists who have described… 'How will the world end.' Hypothesis — Some may be right, some may be wrong. But either the world will perish or the world will live forever. Both cannot take place simultaneously – It is unscientific. But this is exactly what the Bible says. It is mentioned in the Bible in the book of Hebrews, Ch. No.1 Verses No.10 and 11, and the book of Psalms, Ch. No.102, Verse No.25 and 26, that… 'Almighty God created the Heavens and the Earth, and they will perish.' Exactly opposite is mentioned in the book of Ecclesiastics, Ch. No.1, Verse No.4, and the book of Psalms, Ch. No.78, Verse No.69, that… 'The earth will abide forever.'

60

THE BIBLE SAYS THAT THE HEAVENS AND EARTH HAVE PILLARS

I leave it to Dr. William Campbell to choose which of the two Verses are unscientific—the first pair or the second pair. One has to be unscientific, and both cannot take place. The world cannot abide forever as well as perish – It is unscientific. Regarding 'the Heavens', the Bible says in Job, Ch. 26, Verse 11, that… '*The pillars of the Heaven will tremble.*' The Qur'an says in Surah Luqman, Ch. 31, Verse No.10, that… 'The Heavens are without any pillars' - Don't you see? The Bible says that Heavens have got pillars. Not only do the Heavens have pillars but the Bible also says in the first book of Samuel, Ch. No.2 Verses No.8, as well as the book of Job Ch. No.9, Verse No.6, and the book of Psalms Ch. No.75, Verse No.3, that… 'Even the earth have got pillars.' In the field of 'Diet and Nutrition' let's analyse, what does the Bible say. The Bible says in the book of Genesis, Ch. No.1, Verse No.29, that… 'God has given you all the herbs bearing seeds, the trees bearing fruits - those that bear seed, as meat for you.' New International Version says… 'The seed bearing plants, and the trees bearing fruits bearing seeds are food for you, all of them.'

Today, even a layman knows that there are several poisonous plants like wild berries, stritchi, dhatura, plants containing alkaloid, polyander, bacaipoid which if you ingest, there are high possibilities that you may die. How come the Creator of the universe and the human beings do not know that if you have these plants, you will die.

I hope Dr. William Campbell does not give these vegetarian diets to his patients. The Bible has a scientific test how to identify a true believer. It is mentioned in the Gospel of Mark, Ch. No.16, Verse

No.17 and 18 where it says that... 'There will be signs for true believers and among the signs - In my name they shall cast out devils, they shall speak foreign tongues, new tongues, they shall take up serpents - And if they drink deadly poison, they shall not be harmed - And when they place their hand over the sick, they shall be cured.' This is a scientific test. In scientific terminology, it is known as the 'Confirmatory Test' for a true Christian believer. In the past 10 years of my life, I have personally interacted with thousands of Christians, including missionaries, but I have not come across even a single Christian, who has passed this confirmatory test of the Bible. I have not come across a single Christian who took poison, and I have not come across anyone who took poison and did not die. And in scientific terminology, this is also called as the 'Falsification Test' that means if a false person tries and does this test (takes poison), he will die. And a false person will not dare attempt this test. If you are not a true Christian believer, you will not dare attempt this test. Because you try and attempt the falsification test, you will fail. So, a person who is not a true Christian believer will never attempt this test.

I have read the book '**The Qur'an and the Bible : In the light of history and science**' written by Dr. William Campbell. And I assume that he is a true Christian believer, and at least, I would like him to confirm to me about the falsification test. Please be rest assured. I will not ask Dr. William Campbell to have deadly poison, because I don't want to jeopardise the debate. What I'll do - I will only ask him to speak in foreign tongues... in new languages. And as many of you may be aware that India is a land, which has more than 1000 languages and dialects. Only thing I request him is, to say these 3 words... 'One hundred rupees' in the 17 official languages. There are only 17 official languages in India and to make it easier for Dr. William Campbell, I have got a 'One hundred-rupee note.' And this has all the 17 languages mentioned here. Besides English and Hindi, I will help him. I give him a beginning – '*Ek sau rupaiya*' in Hindi. The remaining 15 languages are here; I request him to read.

I know the test says… 'They will speak foreign languages on their own, without the help of reading', but I want to make the test easier, I want to see someone passing the test — I've not seen any one. So if he cannot say it on his own or from his memory, at least read it. I don't mind, I'll accept it. And I would request the chairperson to give it to Dr. William Campbell. He has his rebuttal — 15 languages, '*Ek sau rupaiya*'… 3 words only.

What does the Bible say regarding 'Hydrology'? The Bible says in Genesis, Ch. No.9, Verse No.13 to 17, that… 'After God, at the time of Noah submerged the world by flood, and after the flood' subsided, He said… 'I put up a rainbow in the sky as a promise to the humankind never to submerge the world again, by water'. To the unscientific person, it may be quite good… 'Oh rainbow is a sign of Almighty God, never to submerge the world by flood again.' But today we know very well, that rainbow is due to the refraction of sunlight, with rain or mist. Surely, there must have been thousands of rainbows before the time of Noah, Peace be upon him. To say it was not there before Noah's time and you have to assume that the law of refraction did not exist — which is unscientific.'

WHAT THE BIBLE SAYS ABOUT THE WAY OF DISINFECTING

In the field of medicine, the Bible says in the book of Leviticus,

Ch. No.14, Verse No.49 to 53 - it gives a novel way for disinfecting a house from plague of leprosy... It says that... 'Take two birds, kill one bird, take wood, scale it—and the other living bird, dip it into water... and under running water - later on sprinkle the house 7 times with it. Sprinkle the house with blood to disinfect against plague of leprosy? You know blood is a good media of germs, bacteria and toxin. I hope Dr. William Campbell does not use this method of disinfecting in the OT— the operation theatre.

It is mentioned in the book of Leviticus, Ch. No.12, Verse No.1 to 5, and we know medically, that after a mother gives birth to a child, the post-portal period, it is unhygienic. To say it is 'unclean'. Religiously, I have got no objection. But Leviticus, Ch. No.12 Verse No.1 to 5. says that... 'After a woman gives birth to a male child, she will be unclean for 7 days, and the period of uncleanliness will continue for 33 days more. If she gives birth to a female child, she will be unclean for two weeks, and the period of uncleanliness will continue for 66 days'. In short, if a woman gives birth to a male child... 'a son', she is unclean for 40 days. If she gives birth to a female child... 'a daughter', she is unclean for 80 days. I would like Dr. William Campbell to explain to me scientifically, how come a woman remains unclean for double the period if she gives birth to a female child as compared to a male child.

The Bible also has a very good test for adultery. How to come to know a woman has committed adultery, in the book of Numbers, Ch. no.5 Verse No.11 to 31. I'll just say in brief. It says that... 'The priest should take holy water in a vessel, take dust from the floor, and put it into the vessel - And that is the bitter water 'And after cursing it, give it to the woman And if the woman has committed adultery, after she drinks it, the curse will enter her body, the stomach will swell, the thigh will rot, and she shall be

64

cursed by the people'. If the woman has not committed adultery, she will remain clean and she will bear the seed'. It is projected as a novel method of identifying whether a woman has committed adultery or not.

THE 'BITTER WATER TEST' TO DETECT THE COMMITMENT OF ADULTERY IS BASED ON ABSURDITY

You know today in the world, there are thousands of cases pending in different parts of the world, in different courts of law - only on the assumption that someone has alleged that a woman has committed adultery. I had read in the newspapers, and I came to know from the media that the President of this great country Mr. Bill Clinton was involved in a sex scandal about 2 years back. I wonder why did not the American court use this 'Bitter Water Test' for adultery? He would have gone scot-free immediately. Why did not the Christian missionaries of this great country, especially those who are in the medical field like my respected Dr. William Campbell, use this bitter water test to bail out their President immediately?

'Mathematics' is a branch, which is closely associated to science, with which you can solve problems etc. There are thousands of contradictions in the Bible, and hundreds deal with mathematics. I'll first touch on few of them. It is mentioned in Ezra, Ch. No.2, Verse No.1, and Nehemiah, Ch. No.7, Verse No.6, the context that... 'When the people returned from exile, from Babylon, when king Nebucheldeser of Babylon released the men from Israel, they came back from captivity' - and the list of the people are given. The list is given in Ezra, Ch. No.2, Verse No.2 to 63, and Nehemiah Ch. No.7, Verse No.7 up to 65; the list is given with the names as well as the number of people, having been released.

65

In these 60 Verses, there are no less than 18 times - the name is exactly the same but the number is different. There are no less than 18 contradictions in less than 60 Verses of these two Chapters. This is the list - I don't have time to run through the list. There are no less than 18 different contradictions in less than 60 Verses. Further, it is mentioned in Ezra, Ch. No.2 Verse No.64 that... 'The total congregation, if you add up, it comes to 42,360.' And if you read in Nehemiah, Ch. No.7, Verse No.66, there also the total is the same 42,360. But if you add up all these verses— which I had to do my homework —this is the list of Ezra Ch. No 2, Nehemiah Ch. No 7 - It does not come to 42,360 rather it comes to 29,818. And if you add up Nehemiah, Ch. No. 7, even then, it does not come to 42,360—It comes to 31,089.

The author of the Bible, presumed to be 'Almighty God', does not know simple addition. If you give this problem, even to a person who has passed elementary school, he would be able to get the right answer. If you add up all the 60 Verses, it is so easy. Almighty God did not know adding – *Nauzubillah*—if we presume that this is the word of God.

Further if we read in Ezra Ch. No. 2, Verse No. 65, it says...'There were 200 singing men and women'—Nehemiah Ch. No. 7, Verse No. 67...'There were 245 singing men and women.' Were they 200 — or were they 245 singing men and women? Context is the same i.e. a mathematical contradiction. It is mentioned in the 2nd Kings, Ch. No 24, Verse No 8, that...'Jehoiachin was 18 years old, when he began to reign Jerusalem, he reigned for 3 months and 10 days. 2nd Chronicles, Ch. No 36, Verse No 9, says that...'Jehoiachin was 8 years old when he began to reign and he reigned for 3 months, 10 days'. Was Jehoiachin 18 years when he began to reign or was he 8 years old? Did he reign for 3 months or for 3 months 10 days?

Further, it is mentioned in the 1st Kings, Ch. No 7, Verse No 26, that...'In Solomon's temple, in his molten sea, he had 2000 baths'. In 2nd Chronicles, Ch. No 4, Verse No. 5, he had 3000 baths. Did he have 2000 baths or did he have 3000 baths? That I leave it upon Dr. William Campbell to decide which is correct. There is a clear-cut mathematical contradiction.

Furthermore, it is mentioned in the First Kings, Ch. No. 15, Verse No. 33, that... 'Basha died in the 26th year of reign of Asa.' And 2nd Chronicles Ch. No 16, Verse No 1, says that...'Basha invaded Judah in the 36th years of the reign of Asa.' How can Basha invade 10 years after his death? It is unscientific. I have raised it to make it easier for Dr. William Campbell to answer to the points. I have just mentioned it in brief. The first point was on the 'the creation of the Earth and the Heaven - the universe was in six, 24-hour days. Point No.3. Light was then before the source of light — Point No. 3. Three — Day came into existence before creation of the Earth. Point No. 4 — Earth came into existence before the Sun. Point No. 5 — Vegetation came into existence, before sunlight Point No. 6 — Light of the moon is its own light. Point No. 7 — The earth —Will it perish or will it abide forever? Point No. 8 — The earth has got pillars. Point No. 9 — The heavens have got pillars. Point No. 10 - God said... 'You can have all plants and all vegetation, including the poisonous plants' Point No. 11— The scientific test the falsification test, of Mark, Ch. No. 16, Verse No. 17 and 18. Point No. 12—A woman remains unclean for double the period, if she gives birth to a daughter as compared to a son. Point No. 13 — Using blood to

disinfect the house against plague of leprosy. Point No. 14 —
How do you find out the bitter water test for adultery? Point No.
15—Eighteen different contradictions in less than 60 Verses of
Ezra, Ch. 2, and Nehemiah, Ch. 7. I did not count them as 18
different — I counted them only as one. Point No. 16 — The
total is different is both the chapters. Point No. 17— Are there
200 singing men and women, or are there are 245 singing men
and women? Point No. 18 — Was Jehoiachin 18 years old or
was he 8 years old when he began to reign? Point No. 19 — Did
he reign for 3 months or 3 months 10 days. Point No. 20 — Did
Solomon have 3000 baths or 2000 baths? Point No. 21—Is that
Basha, how could he invade Judah 10 years after his death? Point
No. 22 is —Almighty God — He said, I put up a rainbow in the
sky as a promise to the humankind, never to submerge the world
again by water.

I have listed only 22 points, out of the hundreds available unscientific
points in the Bible... scientific errors. And I request Dr. William
Campbell to answer them. And irrespective of whether he uses
the 'concordance approach' or the 'conflict approach'... as long
as he is logical, he will never be able to prove scientifically, all
these 22 aspects I have told him.

We agree in Jesus Christ Peace be upon him – that the Injeel was
revealed to him. This is not the Injeel. It may contain part of God,
but the other unscientific portion is not the word of God. I would
like to end my talk by giving the quotation of the Glorious Qur'an
from Surah Baqarah, Ch. No. 2, Verse 79 which says: 'Woe to
those who write the book with their own hands, and then say this
is from Allah, to traffic with it for a miserable price. Woe to those
for what they write, woe to those for what they earn.'

Dr. Mohammed requests the audience to maintain due decorum for the continuation of the dialogue and calls upon Dr. William Campbell to present his response to Dr. Zakir Naik.

Dr. William Campbell starts saying, Well! Dr. Naik has brought up some real problems, and there are also the problems, which he has said about. I do not deny them, and I don't have good answers for them. But I will tell about that we are going to make a mathematical study of prophecies - called the theory of probabilities. We will estimate the possibility that these prophecies could be fulfilled by chance.

Dr. Mohammed calls upon Dr. Zakir Naik to present his response to Dr. William Campbell. And then, Dr. Zakir responds: Dr. William Campbell only touched on 2, out of the 22 points I made. You can only solve 2 problems. The 'six day creation problem', and 'first day light came', and 'the third day, Earth', but the remaining four problems are yet to be solved. So Dr. William Campbell chose to say 'Days are long period'- and out of 6, he solved 2 scientific errors. He does not agree to the remaining 4 of 'the creation of the universe'. That is good.

The King James Version as well as the New International Version, which Dr. William Campbell refers to… 'Drink deadly poison' – 'Not eat'… 'Drink.' Dr. William Campbell does not know that there are Indians out here. Surely, many of them may know Gujarati and Marathi; even I know. If I ask you… 'Shu chhe?' Dr. William Campbell did not reply to my 20 points, and he started speaking about 'Prophesy.' What has 'Prophesy' to do with 'Science in the Bible?' If 'Prophesy' is the test - But even if there is one unfulfilled prophesy, the whole Bible is disproved to the word of God.

I can give you a list of unfulfilled prophecies. According to your theory i.e. the 'theory of probability', the Bible is not the word of God. Irrespective of whether you use the 'conflict approach' or the 'concordance approach', if you are logical, you will not be able to take out a single Verse of the Qur'an, which is contradicting. Neither a single Verse is against the established science. If Dr. William Campbell cannot understand the Qur'an, that does not mean that the Qur'an is wrong. The Bible says in Job, Ch. No. 10, Verse No. 9 and 10 that... *We have made the human beings from clay, like poured out milk and curdled cheese.* 'Poured out milk and curdled cheese'... is the exact plagiarisation from the Hippocrates.

I would like to pose this question, or rather this test to Dr. William Campbell. Why don't you attempt the falsification test of the Bible, given in the book of Mark, Ch. 16, Verses 17 and 18, and prove to the audience here right now that you are a true Christian believer?

Dr. Campbell says: My question to Dr. Zakir Naik is that the Christians explain the concept of 'trinity' scientifically by giving the example of water, which can be in their states— solid, liquid and gas, in the form of ice, water and vapour. Similarly, one God is a triune God - Father, Son and the Holy Ghost. Is this explanation scientifically correct?

Dr. Zakir replies that the word 'trinity' is not there in the Bible, but it is there is the Qur'an.

Dr. Campbell says: Dr. Zakir, you said, there is no mistake in the Qur'an. I see more than 20 mistakes in Arabic grammar, and I will tell you some of them. He said in Surah Baqarah. And then in Surah Haj... Which is right—'assabeun' or 'assabreen.' 'Number 1 and number 2'... He said in Surah Taha, 63. Can you explain that?

THE BIBLE IS UNSCIENTIFIC AND NOT FROM GOD

Dr. Zakir remarks that the book he (Dr. Campbell) is referring to is by Abdul Faadi. He then asks, 'Is the Qur'an infallible?' Dr. Campbell, since you are a medical doctor, could you please explain scientifically the various medical aspects, that in the Bible, regarding them, because you did not answer them in your rebuttal. For example, blood is used as a disinfectant, Bitter Water Test for adultery, and most importantly, that the woman is unclean for double the period when she gives birth to a daughter than as compared to a son. Okay Dr. Campbell, if you cannot answer the contradictions in Genesis regarding the 'Creation', don't you think it proves that the Bible is unscientific and therefore, not from God?

Dr. Campbell replies, 'I admit that I have some problems with this'.

Dr. Zakir says, The Muslim yardstick is the Qur'an, which is far superior to your yardstick, the science. Therefore, you should believe in the Qur'an, which is far superior.

Dr. Campbell admits, I agree with Dr. Naik that the errors he has shown are not wrong, and that he cannot answer them. So, does this mean that Dr. Campbell agrees that the Bible has errors - so it is not the word of God? There are the things in the Bible that I cannot explain and I do not have any answer for now.

Dr. Zakir Naik starts with an interrogative sentence, How can a son be two years older than the father? Believe me, even in Hollywood film, you will not be able to produce it.

Dr. Mohammed calls upon Dr. William Campbell to present his response to Dr. Zakir Naik, and Dr. Campbell resumes his speech, saying, Well, Dr. Naik has brought up some real problems. I do not agree to his answer about the Qur'an in terms of the Alaqa

71

and mudgha as I still think it is a big problem. But that is his opinion and my opinion. So, everybody will have to go home and think about it himself or herself. He spoke about... 'He has not met any person that took the poison test.' I cannot present the person, because he has already gone to be with the Lord.

But I have a friend, Harry Rancliff who lived in a town in the South of Morocco and one of his people who he thought was a friend, invited him over for a lunch and a dinner. He had invited his wife and son also. So when Harry agreed to go, somebody came and knocked on the door and said... 'The man is gonna poison you.' So they went - Harry took this very verse which you read, and he decided that he should go, because he had said he would. So he went and waited, hoping to find a time when the man brought in the 'Kuskus', he could turn away... the man would go out, and he could turn the 'Kuskus' around. But there was no such time. So he dug in and ate. His wife was also not able to eat much and they had fed their son before they went. But Harry ate, and that night Harry got pains in his stomach, and he had some bleeding - but he lived.

Two days later, he went and knocked on the door. The man came and opened the door, and his face went absolutely white. Harry thanked him for the meal. I thought, so I give you this one example any way. Now you have said that Jesus was sent only to the Jews....'Only go to the Jews and not to the Gentiles. Well, in the Qur'an itself, it talks about Mary - And then she says...'I do not know any man,' in Surah No.19: 21. And then it says that...'Jesus is to be a sign unto men, and a mercy from us.'

In Mathew 4:9...'A lady came and anointed Jesus' feet. He said...'Whenever and wherever this Gospel is preached in the whole world - what this woman has done will be told.' And in

Mathew 28, when Jesus is about to ascend into the Heaven, he says... 'Go into all the world and preach the Gospel.' But this is not a contradiction. He did say to his disciples...'Go only to the Jews' because the Jews were given a certain chance. There is a story in the Bible – should not use the word 'story' I suppose - It was history - Where Jesus came to a fig tree. And the fig tree had brought no fruit for 3 years. And then, it said...'Shall I tear it down?' And then Jesus' answer was...'No - Leave it one more year, and it will fertilise, and see if it brings any fruit.'

This was all a parable about Israel. He had preached them for 3 years and he would preach another half. But then, there are other parables and he told, where he said...'All right - It will be taken away from you...the blessing, and given to the Gentiles.'

Dr. Naik has talked about 'the day' and 'the periods.' 'The day' in the Bible can also have the time of 'a long period' - Doesn't have to be 24 hours as Dr. Bucaille wanted to insist in his book. And I believe that it was long period of time. And there are also the problems that he has said about, and I do not deny them and I do not have good answers for them, but I will tell about them.

Dr. Naik spoke about the two kinds of salt - the sweet water and the salt water. I do not agree to his explanation. The Qur'an says as...'The God has let free the two barriers...two bodies of flowing water, meeting together - Between them is a barrier which they do not transgress'. Then the word used here for 'barrier' is 'barzakh'...means 'interval' which of the favours of thy Lord will you deny.' or 'gap' or 'break' or 'bar' or 'obstruction' or 'isthmus'. The same information is given in Al-Furqan 25:53...'It is He who has let free the two bodies of flowing water, one palatable and sweet, and the other salty and bitter. And He made between them

73

a barrier, and a partition that it is forbidden to pass.' The phrase...'A partition that it is forbidden to pass' represents two words from the same root. This is done in Arabic to stress or accept whatever is being discussed. The word 'hijr' means 'forbidden', 'interdicted', 'prohibited.' All are very strong words. And the second word, which is the last participle of the verb, has the same meanings. Therefore, very literally, one might translate this as...'He, God made between them a bar, and a forbidden...forbidding.' Dr. Bucaille discusses this briefly and then he says, though he admits at the end. Well, it mixes far out to see. A scientist friend commenting on this, said...'It is simply that the salt and fresh water are physically separated. The effluent from the river displacing the seawater, but there is no barrier. Thermodynamically, the mixing is a spontaneous, immediate process, highly favoured by entropy. The only barrier is canonic. It takes a long time for that much stuff to mix. I myself have had a tiny example of this.

I had a friend in Tunisia who used to hunt for Octopus. So, I went there once, and I jumped out of the boat and began swimming around. It was right at the place, where a small creek came in, and the top water was cold while the bottom water was hot. I thought, how could this be! The top is cold while the bottom is hot? Then I realised that the cold water was coming out of the river, and the salt water is heavy. So the salt water was at the bottom and the cold light water was at the top.

Dr. Naik spoke about the languages. Of course, I am not able to answer about the languages in India. I could not answer about the Indian languages in America either. So, it is no difference between India and America. However, the place that he talks about in the

Bible...the disciples were given languages as a miracle. But they were the many languages that the people who were there knew that they were not weak in the languages that were unknown. If somebody comes from Spain, an apostle speaks to that person in his language from Spain. If another person comes from Turkey, a different apostle speaks to the other person in his language from Turkey. I am going to say something that I had prepared to give, and talk about 'Witnesses.'

In Deuteronomy, God told Moses...'The way to know true Prophet was—Did his prophecy come true?'—Elijah is an example. Elias in the Qur'an went to the king and told him...'It is not going to rain till I say so.' And so, for 6 months there was no rain, and then year spent, yet there was no rain. Once in Tunisia, there was a whole year and no rain fell there. Then 2 years, there was no rain, then 3 years, then 3 and a half years. And then Elaijah went to the king and said...'We gonna have a contest.'—And they went up on Mount Carmel and had this contest—And the king lost.

And in the Qur'an, it says that...*'Elias had waged a wonderful victory. But then Elias fell down on his knees—Elaijah and he prayed for rain and the rain came. Elaijah is the first witness. When he said...'It is not going to rain till I say so'.* He was the first witness. When God made the rain come, when Elaijah fell down on his knees, God Himself was the second witness.

Another example is Isaiah, 750 B.C—The Jews were sent into exile. He prophesied that they would be sent to exile, and then Cyrus would bring them back. Who is Cyrus? 250 years later, Cyrus the Persian Pagan king sent the Jews back to Israel... back to Palestine - And there is a Cyrus cylinder in London that talks Jesus makes prophecies about it. So you can ask a question... 'Did Jesus fulfil prophecies? ...Did Jesus do miracles?

MATHEMATICAL STUDY OF PROPHECIES

We are going to make a mathematical study of Prophesies, which is called the theory of probabilities. And we will estimate the possibility that these prophecies could be fulfilled by chance. An example of this is —Supposing Dr. Naik has ten shirts, and I know he has a red shirt. And I say... 'Tomorrow he is going to wear the red shirt.' And tomorrow he does so, then I say... 'I am a Prophet.' All of my friends is gonna say... 'No, no, that just happened by chance.'

Well then, supposing Dr. Samuel Nauman has two pairs of shoes and a pair of sandals. So then the next day, I prophesise what shirt Dr. Naik is going to wear, and I prophesise that Dr. Samuel Nauman is going to wear his sandals, and Dr. Sabeel Ahmed has 5 hats, and I say he is going to wear his turban. What are the chances that I could have all of these rights, by chance? Anyway, you multiply 1 over 10, by 1 over 5, by 1 over 3, and you get 1 over a hundred and fifty, and that is my chance of getting it by luck. Is it possible to have the slide projected down please? I mean... the screen down? Well, the time is going, and we are going to look at 10 prophecies. And then, the one, which we will not count, because we want to prove it.

The first one is Prophecy in Jeremiah 600 B.C — that the Messiah must be from the posterity of David. 'The days are coming...declares the Lord, when I will raise up to David a righteous friend, a king who will reign wisely and do what is just and right in the land. He will be called the Lord Yahowah or

76

righteousness'. And the fulfilment was in the 6th month - The Angel Gabriel was sent from God to Mary. The Angel said to her: 'Do not be afraid Mary. Behold you will conceive in your womb, and bear a son. He will be called Jesus - He will be great and will be called the son of the Most High. And the Lord God, will give to him the throne of his father David, and in his kingdom there will be no end.' And the Angel said to her... 'The Holy Spirit will come upon you, and the power of the Most High will overshadow you. Therefore, the child to be born will be called holy'.

Well, when David was first, he was just from a small family. But after he became king, and his family was known, everybody would remember that there was a fifth cousin of the king. So, I am going to assume that 1 in 200 Jewish people belonged to the family of David.

The second prophecy is everlasting ruler to be born in Bethlehem. Micah, 750 B.C... 'But you O Bethlehem, Ephrathah who are little to be among the clans of Judah - from you shall come forth for me, one who is to be ruler in Israel—whose origin is from of old from ancient days.' And the fulfilment—Though Joseph and Mary lived in Nazareth, because of an order from Ceaser Agustus, Joseph had to take Mary to Bethlehem, his native town. In the fulfilment it says... 'And Joseph also went up from Galilee, from the city of Nazareth, to Judea, to the city of David, which is called Bethlehem — because he was of the house and lineage of David. And while there, she gave birth to her first born son'. Well, what is the chance of being born in Bethlehem? There are about 2 billion people who were born in the world, from Micah until now, and 7000 live in Bethlehem. So one man, out of every 280 thousand men was born in Bethlehem.

The 3rd prophecy – A messenger will prepare the way for the Messiah. This was done by Malachi, in Chapter No. 3:1, in 400 B.C... 'Behold I send my messenger to prepare the way before me — and the Lord whom you seek, will suddenly — come to his temple. The messenger of the covenant is in whom you delight - Behold he is coming, says the Lord of hosts.' The fulfilment - The next day - John the Baptist... Yahya ibn Zakariya saw Jesus coming toward him and said... 'Behold the Lamb of God, who takes away the sin of the world!' This is he of whom I said... 'After me comes a man who ranks before me - for he was before me.' And to this, the Qur'an agrees also in the story of, The Family of Imran, 3:39 - 45, when it says... 'Yahya is to come witnessing the truth of a word from God whose name will be Christ Jesus, the son of Mary.' How many leaders had a forerunner? It is hard to say. I put down 1 man in a 1000 was a leader, who had a forerunner.

The fourth prophecy is that Messiah would do many signs and miracles. In Isaiah, 750 we read... 'Say to those with fearful hearts - Be strong and do not fear - Your God will come and he will save you. Then will the eyes of the blind be opened, and the ears of the deaf be unstopped, then will the lame leap like a deer, and the tongue of the dumb, shout for joy'. The fulfilment: The Gospel states, as does the Qur'an, that Jesus did many miracles.

The Bible speaks of only 4 Prophets who did many miracles — Moses, Elaijah, Elaisha and Jesus. Jesus is the only one who did all four types of miracles as mentioned in the prophecy, and he sometimes healed all, who came to him. Since many Muslims believe that there were 1,24,000 Prophets, we will use that number and say that Jesus was the one man among 1,24,000.

The fifth Prophecy: In spite of these signs, his brothers were against him. In the song of David, a 1000 B.C, he says… 'I have become a stranger to my brother, an alien to my mother's sons'. And in John, he gives the fulfilment… 'So his brothers said to him leave here and go to Judeo for even his brothers did not believe in him.' A question might be - One ruler in how many will have found his family against him? Many kings were overthrown by their own relatives. Therefore, we will say, 1 in 5, or 2 times 10 to the first power.

And the **6th Prophecy:** It is given by Zakaria in 520 B.C… 'Rejoice straightly, O daughter of Zion shout, O daughter of Jerusalem. Behold your king come unto you: he is just and having salvation — lowly and riding upon an ass.' The fulfilment… 'The next day, the great crowd took some palm branches and went out to meet him shouting, Hosanna. Blessed is he who comes in the name of the Lord! Blessed is the king of Israel! And Jesus found a young donkey and sat upon it.

Obviously, Jesus chose to sit upon the donkey, and that is not a miracle. It is nothing unusual. But the crowd was there and the crowd came and praised him and said… 'Blessed is he who comes in the name of the Lord.' How many rulers entered Jerusalem on a donkey? Nowadays he comes in a Mercedes. I said, one ruler in a hundred.

The Seventh prophecy: Jesus foretells the destruction of the temple and he himself gave the prophecy. So, Jesus said this sometime in 30 A.D. And as he was going out of the temple, one of his disciples said to him… 'Stones, and what wonderful buildings.' And Jesus' Teacher, behold what wonderful said to him… 'Do you see these great buildings? Not one stone shall be left upon another, which will not be thrown down.' In the fulfilment:

About 40 years later in 70 A.D, the Roman General Titus captured Jerusalem after a long siege. Titus had intended to spare the temple, but the Jews set it on fire. For the Jews to revolt and then be crushed would be common. So I said 1 chance in 5.

For **The eighth prophecy** - The Messiah will be crucified. In Psalms, David wrote in 1000 B.C...'A band of evil men has encircled me - They have pierced my hand and my feet.' Well, Jesus... David did not die this way. He died in his bed. His feet and hands were not pierced. Luke gives us the fulfilment...'When they came to the place called 'The skull', there they crucified Jesus along with the criminals — One on his right, the other on his left.' Our question is — One man in how many, has been crucified? I said, one man in 10,000.

The ninth prophecy — They will divide his garments, and cast lot for his robe. Again, David is speaking...'They divided my garments among them, and cast lots for my clothing.' John gives us the fulfilment in Chapter 19...'When the soldiers crucified Jesus, they took his clothes, dividing them into four shares, one for each of them, with the under garment remaining. This garment was seamless, woven in one piece, from top to bottom. Let's not tear it; they said, Let's decide by lot who will get it'. How many criminals would have a seamless garment? Well, you can make your own decision, but I said one in a 100.

The 10th prophecy – 'Though innocent, he would be counted with the wicked and with the rich in his death. Isaiah said in 750 B.C...'He was assigned a grave, with the wicked and with the rich in his death. Though he had done no violence nor was any deceit in his month, he was numbered with the transgressors.' Mathew gives the fulfilment...'They crucified two robbers with

80

him. As evening approached, there came a rich man from Arimathea, named Joseph - a disciple of Jesus. Going to Pilate, he asked for Jesus' body. Joseph wrapped it in a clean linen cloth and placed it in his own tomb'.

How many executed criminals were innocent? I said, one man in 10. And how many innocent men or how many criminals were buried with the rich? I said, one man in a hundred. That gives 1 in a thousand. Finally, the prophecy... After dying, he will rise from the dead. In Isaiah again, it says... 'For he was cut off from the land of the living. He died, and though the Lord makes his life guilt offering, he will see his offspring and prolong his days. So there is a prophecy, that he will come back to life. Luke tells us Jesus himself stood among them and said to them... 'Peace be with you.' And then Paul gives us a summary in 1st Corinthians 15, that Jesus appeared to Peter and then to the twelve. After that, he appeared to more than 500 of the brothers at the same time, most of who are still living - then to James— Jesus' half brother and then to all the apostles. That is not something you can give a value to.

So, now we are going to look at the calculation. One man in how many men the world over, will fulfil all the ten prophecies? This question can be answered by multiplying all of our estimates. I do not have time to read them but the answer is one chance in 2 times. 2.78 times 10, to the 28.28 zeros. Let's simplify and reduce the number by calling it 1 time 10 to the 28.

The best information available in the case of number of men who ever lived to be is about 88 billion. We call that, 1 time 10 to the eleven. By dividing these two numbers, we find that the chance that any man might have lived down to the present time, and fulfilled

81

all the 10 prophecies by luck is 1 in 10 to the 17. That is written out this way, with seventeen zeroes.' Let's try and imagine this. If you took to the state of Texas and you covered it with dollar coins, one meter deep, 3 feet deep, several dollars, and then one coin was marked electrically. And then I say there, go and walk out into the state of Texas and pick the right coin. That is your chance of picking the right coin by chance. In other words, it is no chance.

I am having a trouble. There are many more prophecies, which show Prophet David or Isaiah the first witness — God causing fulfilment, is the second witness. And God caused the disciples of Jesus to write it down. These are all proofs that the Bible is true and from Yehowah Elohim. The Gospel says that…'Jesus came from God, and paid the penalty for our sins' This is good news. The Qur'an has hard news —Surah Nahl 16:61 says…'*If Allah were to punish men for their wrongdoing, He will not leave on earth, a single living creature.*'

The problem is that the Qur'an states very clearly that even those who have done their best are given only a 'may be.' In the Surah of the Narration, Al-Qasas it says… '*Perhaps for him who shall repent, and believe and do right, perhaps 'asahan'…he may be one of the successful.*' In 'The Forbidding'…Al-Tahrim it says…'*O you who believe, repent toward Allah with a sincere repentance - It maybe that your Lord would get back from you, your evil deeds.*' In the Surah of 'Repentance' – 'Al Tauba', it says…'*Those only shall worship in the mosques of Allah, who believe in Allah and the last day, and observe proper worship, and give alms and fear none except Allah, and it might be that these are the rightly guided.*'

At the end, it is very lonely if a person does not believe, then he is sure to go to hell. But if he does believe on the Day of Judgement, he stands there all by himself in front of Allah. There is no intercessor or friend, and he can only hope that, may be, perhaps, he might be among the blessed. This is hard news wherein if this dictionary translates, 'al asahan', 'it might be', 'it could be', 'that, possibly', 'may be', 'perhaps.'

In the Oxford dictionary, English to Arabic, 'perhaps' is translated as 'asahan' — this may be true but it is hard. On the other hand, the Gospel has good news. Jesus said...'I did not come to be served, but to serve - to give my life a ransom for many'. Another Verse from Paul the apostle says...'If you confess with your mouth that Jesus is Lord, and believe in your heart that God raised him from the dead, you will be saved straight out'. This is wonderful good news. You read with me these fulfilled prophecies as proofs.

There were 500 people who saw Christ, after he rose from the dead. There are many archaeological findings, confirming the Bible. I urge you to get a copy of the Bible of the Gospel and read it. You will find good news for your soul. May God bless you all! Thank you.

Dr. Mohammed calls upon Dr. Zakir Naik to present his response to Dr. William Campbell. Dr. Zakir Naik starts with the words of greetings and salams to all present there, and then he says:

Dr. William Campbell only touched on 2, out of the twenty-two points I made. The first point he raised was he thinks that 'the days' mentioned in the Bible refer to long periods. I already gave the reply in my talk that if you consider 'days' to be 'long periods', like the Qur'an, you can only solve two problems. The 'six-day

83

creation problem, and 1st day light came, and 3rd day earth.' The remaining four problems, yet are there. So Dr. William Campbell chose to say... 'Days are long period.' And out of 6, he solved only 2 scientific errors. The remaining four... 'Of the creation of the universe, he does agree it. That is good. And he says it is difficult to answer.

The second point he touched on, was regarding the scientific test of Mark Chapter No 16, Verse No 17 & 18, and he said... 'One of his friend named Harry, whatever the name was, in Morocco ate '*khuskhus.*' The Bible says, the King James Version as well as the New International Version which Dr. William Campbell refers to 'drink deadly poison'... not eat – 'drink.' Yet, I do not mind - Even if a person eats deadly poison also, no problem. But imagine one man in Morocco I am told there are 2 billion Christians in the world, and no one can come forward, one out of the 2 billion? I thought Dr. William Campbell was a true Christian believer, and I asked him to pass the test not to his friend, who already died.

Dr. Campbell said that... 'Blood came out of the mouth.' Being medical doctors, both Dr. William Campbell and even myself know very well that in the case of having poison, blood comes out, and we cure many people of poison. So, what is so great about this test? You should come forward and do all these things, and yet you should be able to speak foreign tongues.

And Dr. William Campbell said that at that time if you read Gospel of Mark, Chapter 16, those people there, they spoke the languages people knew, and foreign tongues. Dr William Campbell does not know there are Indians out here - Surely many may know Gujarati, Marathi - even I know. If I ask you... '*Shu Cheh*? Suppose if I ask you in a particular language... *'Neer kud'*. *'Neer Kud'* ...(in Tamil), no reply will come. Foreign tongues... *'Neer Kud'*. Anyone knows Tamil or Malalayam?

One fellow from the audience raised the hands with affirmation, and Dr. Zakir Naik spoke to him:

Yes, very good! Are you a Christian believer? ... No I am asking that person there; you are a Muslim? Anyway fine, this was supposed to be a test passed by the Christian believers. There are many people who know foreign languages out here. Only thing you had to do was speak to them like...'What is your name? ... How are you? For example, *'Kaifa haaluka'* in Arabic, which you know - New languages which you did not know and you have proved my point. And yet, I have not come across a single Christian, who has passed this test in front of me - Not a single, out of the thousands I have met personally. And now it can be 1001, after meeting Dr. William Campbell - Only touched two points.

Dr William Campbell did not reply to my twenty points, and he started speaking about 'Prophecy.' What has 'Prophecy' to do with science in the Bible? If 'Prophecy' is the test, then Nostradamus' book should be the best book to be called...'the Word of God' - It is right. He spoke about the 'Theory of probability.'

IF THERE IS ONE UNFULFILLED PROPHECY, THE WHOLE BIBLE IS DISPROVED TO BE THE WORD OF GOD

For the definition of 'Theory of probability' - how you can analyse with the Qur'an with scientific facts, refer to my video cassette, **'Is the Qur'an God's word.'** It is available in the foyer. I have

85

proved scientifically, how can you use 'Theory of probability.' Dr. William Campbell used it on the basis of 'Prophecy.' If I want, I can try and prove his prophecies wrong, but I do not want to do it. I will take it for granted for the sake of argument, using the concordance approach that whatever prophecies he said, was right - for the sake of argument. But even if there is one unfulfilled prophecy, the whole Bible is disproved to be the word of God.

I can give you a list of unfulfilled prophecies. For example if you read Genesis, Chapter No. 4, Verse No. 12, it says... 'God told Cain: You will never be able to settle; you will be a wanderer.' Few Verses later on Genesis, Chapter No.4, Verse No.17, says...'Cain built up a city' – unfulfilled prophecy. If you read Jeremiah, Chapter No.36, Verse No.30, it says that...'Jehoiachin the father of Jehoiachin... no one will be able to sit on his throne - The throne of David, no one will be able to sit after Jehoiachin.' If you read later on, II Kings, Chapter No 24, Verse No 6, it says that... 'Jehoiachin after he died, later on Jehoiachin sat on the throne' - Unfulfilled prophecy. One is sufficient to prove it is not the word of God. I can give plenty of references.

If you read Ezekiel, Chapter No 26, it says that...'Nebuchader, he will destroy Tyre.' We come to know that Alexander the great was the person who destroyed Tyre - Unfulfilled prophecy. Isaiah, Chapter No. 7, Verse No 14, says, prophesying of...'The coming of a person who will be born to a virgin - his name shall be Emmanuel.' They say... the Christians - it refers to Jesus Christ Peace be upon him. Born to a virgin - the Hebrew word there is 'amla', which means not 'a virgin'- 'a young lady.' The word for 'virgin' in Hebrew is 'baitula', which is not there. Even if you agree, we are using concordance. We agree to the word, 'Virgin'

- No problem. It says... 'He will be called Emanuel.' Nowhere in the Bible is Jesus Christ Peace be upon him, called as Emmanuel - Unfulfilled prophecy.

I can give several unfulfilled prophecies - One is sufficient to prove the Bible wrong though I have given a few. According to your theory of probability, the Bible is not the word of God. Dr. William Campbell said that... 'According to the Qur'an, Elaijah won the battle. According to the Bible, Elaijah lost the battle' - Whatever it is. That does not mean that the Bible is correct and the Qur'an is wrong. If the statements differ in the Bible and the Qur'an, you are assuming the Bible the word of God. If both are supposed to be analysed, it can be possible that the Qur'an is right, and the Bible is wrong. It can be possible the Bible is right, and the Qur'an is wrong. It can be possible both are wrong. It can be possible both are right. So what we have to do, if we have to analyse which of the two is wrong, you have to get a third source from outside, which is authentic. Just because the Bible says... 'Elaijah lost' - and the Qur'an says... 'Elaijah won'. Therefore, the Qur'an is wrong – it is illogical.

Dr. William Campbell! Besides replying to scientific errors, I had mentioned that I would just touch on the points, which I could not do due to lack of time. There are an additional 6 or 7 points, which he has mentioned in his talk, to which Insha-Allah I will give the reply briefly. He spoke that the Qur'an says...according to me - and he showed my cassette according to Br. Shabbir Ali that... 'The light of the moon is reflected light.' And he said... 'It doesn't mean that.'

ALLAH HAS GOT THE LIGHT OF HIS OWN

I am quoting again; the Qur'an mentions in Surah Furqan, Chapter No.25, Verse No.61 that... 'Blessed is He who has placed in the

87

sky constellation, placed there in lamp… 'Sun' and 'moon' having 'borrowed light'… '*Munir*.' The Arabic word used for 'moon' is '*Qamar*' - It is always described as '*Munir*' or '*Nur*' meaning 'reflection of light.' The Arabic word used for 'sun' is '*Shams*' - It is always described as 'wahad' 'dia', which means 'a blazing torch', 'A shining glory.' And I can give references from the Surah Nur, Chapter No.71 Verse.15 and 16, Surah Yunus, Chapter No.10 Verse No.5 and so on. And he said that if it means 'a reflection of light', - and he quoted the Qur'an, Surah Al-Nur Chapter No.24, Verse No.35 and 36 that… '*Allah Subhanahu-wa-taala* is '*Nuras samawati wal ard*'. '**Is the light of the heavens and the earth.**' Read the complete verse, and analyse what does it says. It says… '**Allah is the light**'… '*Nur.*' It says… '**Allah is the light of the Heavens and the Earth.**'

It is a similitude - like a niche, and within the niche there is lamp. The 'lamp' word is there. So *Allah Subhanahu-wa-taala* has got light of His own, and even reflected light. Like you see a halogen lamp - you know which are here. The lamp inside is like a 'siraj' but the reflector is like moon. It is reflecting light. The lamp and the tube are having a light of their own, but the reflector of the halogen lamp is reflecting light – Thus, both two in one. So *Allah Subhanahu-wa-taala, Alhamdulillah*…besides having light of His own - as the Qur'anic verse says… In the niche there is a lamp, and that lamplight of *Allah Subhanahu-wa-taala* is His own light, and Allah reflects His own light.

Dr. William Campbell says that… 'The Qur'an says that… 'Qur'an is nur'… It is reflecting light.' Of course, the Qur'an is reflecting the light and the guidance of Allah Subhana-wa-taala.

MUHAMMAD (S.A.W.) IS ALSO '*NUR*' AND '*SIRAJ*'

Regarding Prophet Mohammed Sallallahu alaihi wasallam being *Siraj* - Yes he is. The Hadith of the beloved Prophet (S.A.W.) is giving guidance to us. So Muhammad Sallallahu alaihi wassallam is '*nur*', and also '*Siraj*'- *Alhamdullillah*. He has his own knowledge also. He has the guidance from *Allah Subhanahu-wa-taala*. So if you use the word '*Nur*' as reflected light, and Munir as reflected light, yet *Alhamdulillah* you can prove it scientifically that the light of the moon is not its own light, but it is the reflected light.

The other point, Dr. William Campbell raised was regarding Surah Kahf Chapter No.18, Verse No.86, that... '*Zulqarnain sees the sun setting in murky water... in turbid water - Imagine sun setting in murky water... unscientific.*' The Arabic word used here is 'wajada' meaning '**it appeared to Zulqarnain.**' And Dr. William Campbell knows Arabic. So '*wajada*' means - if you look up in the dictionary also, it means it appeared.' So Allah Subhana-wa-taala is describing what appeared to Zulqarnain.

If I make a statement that... 'The student in the class said, 2 plus 2 is equal to 5.' And you say... 'Oh Zakir said, 2 plus 2 is equal to 5. I did not say. I am telling...'The student in the class said, 2 plus 2 is equal to 5.' I am not wrong - The student is wrong. There are various ways to try and analyse this verse. One is this way - according to Muhammad Asad, 'wajada' means... 'It appeared to'... 'It appeared to Zulqarnain.' Point no.2 - The Arabic word used is 'Maghrib' can be used for time as well as place. When we say 'sunset', it can be taken for time. If I say... 'The sun sets at 7 p.m.' I am using it for time. If I say... 'The 'Sun sets in the West', it means I am taking it for place. So here if we use the word 'Maghrib' for time, Zulqarnain did not reach that place of sunset -

used as time. He reached at the time of sunset. The problem is solved.

Furthermore, you can solve them in various ways. Even if Dr. William Campbell says... 'No no, the basic assumption is too much. It is not... 'Appeared to'... it is actually this.' Let's analyse it further. The Qur'anic verse says... 'The Sun set in murky water.' Now we know, when we use these words, like 'sunrise' and 'sunset' - Does the sun rise? Scientifically, sun does not rise - neither does the sun set. We know scientifically that the sun does not set at all. It is the rotation of the earth, which gives rise to sunrise and sunset. But yet you read in the everyday papers mentioning, sunrise at 6 a.m. sun sets at 7.00 p.m. Oh! The newspapers are wrong – Unscientific!' If I use the word 'Disaster', Oh! There is a disaster' – 'Disaster' means there is some calamity which has taken place. Literally, 'disaster' means 'an evil star.' So when I say... 'This disaster' every one knows what I mean is 'a calamity', not about the evil star.'

Dr. William Campbell and I know, when a person who is mad, we call him a lunatic - Yes or no? At least, I do, and I believe Dr. William Campbell also will be doing that. We call a person 'a lunatic'. What is the meaning of 'lunatic'? It means... 'Struck by the moon', but that is how the language has evolved. Similarly, sunrise is actually just a usage of words. And Allah has given the guidance for the human beings also - He uses so that we understand. So it is just 'sunset' - Not that it is actually setting - Not that sun is actually rising.

Thus, this explanation clearly gives us a clear picture, that the Verse of the Qur'an of Surah Kahf, Chapter.18, Verse No 86, is not in contradiction with established science - That is the way how people speak. He quoted Surah Furqan, Chapter. 25, Verse. 45 and 46, that… 'The shadow lengthens and prolongates - We can make it stationary - the sun is its guide.' And in his book he mentions… 'Does the sun move?' Where does this Verse say 'The sun moves.' The Holy Qur'an in Surah Furqan, Chapter.25, Verse. 45 and 46 does not say that the sun moves.

And he writes in his book… 'We were taught in eliminatory school' - and he said that also in his talk that… 'It is due to the rotation of the earth that the shadow prolongs and gets small, but what the Qur'an says… 'The sun is its guide.' Today, even a person who has not gone to school knows that shadow is due to sunlight. Thus, the Qur'an is perfectly right. It does not say the sun moves and the shadow is caused. He is putting his own words in the Qur'an. The Sun is its guide - It is guiding the shadow. Without sunlight, you cannot have shadow. Yes, you can have shadows of the light - it is a different thing. But here it is referring to the shadow, which you see moving, prolonging and becoming short.

Dr. William Campbell spoke about Solomon's death - Surah Saba, Chapter 34, Verse 12 to 14, and said that… *'Imagine a person standing on the stick, and he dies, and no one comes to know, etc.'* Here are various ways to explain - Point No. 1, Solomon (Peace be upon him), was a Prophet of God, and it can be a miracle.

When the Bible says that Jesus Christ (Peace be upon him), could give life to the dead, Jesus Christ is born of a virgin birth. Which is more difficult to imagine' - Being born of a virgin birth, giving life to the dead or standing on a stick for a very long time? So, when God can do miracles through Jesus Christ Peace is upon him, why cannot he do a miracle through Solomon Alaihissalam. Moosa

(Moses) Alai Salaam parted the sea. He threw a stick, which became a snake – the Bible and the Qur'an say that. So when God can do that, why cannot God let a man rest for a long period?

NOT A SINGLE QUR'ANIC VERSE IS AGAINST THE ESTABLISHED SCIENCE

Anyway, I have given him various different answers. Nowhere does the Qur'an say that Sulaiman Alaihissalam rested on the stick for a very long period. It just says that... animal, some say... 'Ant'... may be other animal of the earth came and bit. It may be possible. May be, that Sulaiman Alaihissalam was just dead, and any animal may have shook the stick, and he may have fallen down. But I assume that I use the conflict approach with the Qur'an, because irrespective of whether you use the conflict approach or the concordance approach, the ayat (Verse) I quoted in the beginning of my talk Surah Nisa, Chapter 4 Verse, 82, says... '*Do they not consider the Qur'an with care?' Had it been from anyone besides Allah, there would have been many contradictions.* Irrespective of whether you use the conflict approach or the concordance approach, if your approach is logical, you will not be able to take out a single Verse of the Qur'an, which is contradicting and there is not a single verse which is against the established science.

JINNS ALSO DO NOT HAVE THE 'ILM-E-GHAIB'— KNOWLEDGE OF THE UNSEEN

I agree with Dr. William Campbell that Sulaiman *Alaihissalam* stayed for a long time. The answer is given in the same verse that after Sulaiman Alaihissalam fell down; the Jinns said that... 'If we would have known that Solomon Peace be upon him died, we would not have toiled so hard.' It indicates that even the Jinns do not have 'Ilm-e-ghaib'; they do not have the knowledge of the unseen. Because, the Jinns thought themselves to be very great - So Allah is teaching them, that even they do not have 'Ilm-e-ghaib'.

IBN NAFEES WAS THE FIRST PERSON TO TELL ABOUT THE CIRCULATION OF BLOOD, 600 YEARS AFTER THE REVELATION OF THE QUR'AN

Dr. William Campbell touched on 'the production of milk', in Surah Nahl, Chapter 16, Verse 66. The first person who told about the circulation of blood, was Ibn Nafees, 600 years after the Revelation of the Qur'an. And 400 years after Ibn Nafees, William Harvey made it common to the Western world - That is 1000 years after the Revelation of the Glorious Qur'an.

THE QUR'AN SAYS ABOUT THE FORMATION AND USAGE OF MILK 1400 YEARS AGO

The food you eat, go into the intestine, and from the intestines, the food constituents reach the various organs via the blood stream; many a times via the portal system of liver, and it even reaches the mammary gland, which is responsible for production of the milk. And the Qur'an gives this information of modern science in a nutshell in Surah Nahl, Chapter. 16, Verse. 66, where it says: *'Verily in the cattle, is a lesson for you. We give you to drink from what is with in their body, coming from a conjunction between the constituent of the intestine and blood - milk which is pure for you to have.'* Alhamdulillah, what we came to know just recently in science means 50 years back, 100 years back while the Qur'an mentions this information 1400 years ago and repeats this message in Surah Muminum, Chapter 23, Verse 21.

93

Dr. William Campbell raised the point on 'Animals living in community.' The Qur'an says in Surah Anam, Chapter 6, Verse. 38...'*We have created every animal that lives on the earth, and every bird that flies in the air, to live in communities, like you.*' And Dr. Campbell says that... 'You know the spider kills the mate and the father etc... do we kill? And the lion does that, and the elephant does that; he is talking about the behaviour. The Qur'an is not referring to behaviour.

If Dr. William Campbell cannot understand the Qur'an, that does not mean that the Qur'an is wrong. The Qur'an says: '**They live in communities**'. It is talking about the animals and the birds, which live in-groups and in societies like the human beings; it is not talking about behaviour.

Today, science tells that all the animals, the birds and the living creatures of the world live in communities. Like the human beings means they live together. And I did not have time to touch on all the points on Embryology. I have touched on all his 8, 9 topics, which he spoke on. Regarding Embryology, I will go more in detail. The points he raised in Embryology besides the one I clarified in my talk. He said that the stages of development were mentioned by Hippocrates and by Gallon, and he showed the various slides. The point to be noted is that just because someone says something, which are matching with the Qur'an that does not mean that the Qur'an has been copied from that.

Suppose I make a statement which is correct, and which was said by somebody else earlier. That does not mean that I have copied. It may be, and it may not be also. To use the conflict approach with the Qur'an we find that it does not take the things which were wrong from Hippocrates. If he had copied, he would have

94

copied everything; it is logical. All the stages of Hippocrates and Gallon are not the same as the Qur'an. Hippocrates and Gallon do not speak about 'leech like substance.' They do not speak about 'mudgha' at all. Where do they speak?

Hippocrates and Gallon at that time said that... 'Even the women have got semen' - who says that? Even the Bible says that. If you read in the Bible, it is mentioned in Leviticus Chapter No.12, Verse No.1 to 12, that woman gives out seed - So actually the Bible is copying from Hippocrates. And the Bible says in Job, Chapter No.10, Verse No.9 and 10, that... 'We have made the human beings from clay, like poured out milk and curdled cheese.' Poured out milk and curdled cheese, is exact plagiarisation from Hippocrates. Why plagiarisation? Because, surely that is not the word of God, and that portion is unscientific.

THE BIBLE COPIES THE HIPPOCRATES AND GALLON

It was said by Hippocrates and Gallon, the Greeks that... 'Human beings are created like curdled cheese', and the Bible copies that exactly. But Qur'an *Alhamdulillah!*

, and if you analyse and read the books on 'Embryology, even of Dr. Keith Moore, he says that... 'Hippocrates and the other people like Gallon etc. did give a lot of things to embryology, initially, as well as Aristotle' - Many were right and many were wrong.' And further, he goes to say... 'In the middle ages or at the time of the Arabs, the Qur'an speaks about something additional.' If it was exactly copied, why would Dr. Keith Moore in his book give due credit to the Qur'an. He even gives due credit to Aristotle and Hippocrates, but mentioned there... 'Many were wrong.' That, he does not mention with the Qur'an. That proof suffices to say that the Qur'an was not copied from the Greek time.

Regarding 'light of the moon.'... 'Light of the moon' was copied from Greeks. You will tell me that... 'The world is spherical' was copied from the Greeks. I know the Pthogorous, the Greeks lived in 6th century B.C who believed that the earth rotated. They believed that the sunlight was reflected. If Prophet Mohammed (S.A.W.)... Nauzubillah... copied, why did not he copy? They believed the sun was stationary and it was the centre of the universe. So why did Prophet Mohammed (S.A.W.) copy the correct thing and delete the things that were not correct? This is sufficient proof that Prophet Mohammed (S.A.W.) did not copy. He goes to give a list that goes from Greek to Cyriac, Cyriac to Arabic... and big research. One statement of the Qur'an is sufficient to disprove it. The Qur'an says in Surah Ankabut, Chapter. 29, Verse No.48, that... 'Thou was not able to recite any book before this, nor was thou able to transcribe with thy right hand.' If it were so, the talkers of vanity would have surely doubted.' The Prophet (S.A.W.) was an 'ummi.' He was an illiterate. This fact of history is sufficient to prove that he did not plagiarise from anywhere. Enough! Imagine! Even a scientist, who is very literate, cannot do this thing. But Allah in his Divine Guidance made the last Prophet (S.A.W.), as an 'ummi' so that the talkers of vanity like the people who write books against Islam, cannot open their mouths.

THE BIBLE IS INCOMPATIBLE WITH THE MODERN SCIENCE

There are various things that I can continue speaking about the Bible. I have covered up all his arguments against the Qur'an... Alhamdulillah, not a single point to prove that the Qur'an is against science. He has not touched on 22 points of mine. Touched on 2

- not proven. So all twenty-two yet to be proved, that the Bible is incompatible with modern science.

Point no.23 - In the field of Zoology, it is mentioned in Leviticus, Chapter No.11 Verse No.6, that… 'Hare is a cud chewier.' We know that hare does not chew cud. Previously, people thought by the movement of the hare. Now we know hare is not a cud chewier, neither does it have a compact mentalised stomach. It is mentioned in the Proverbs, Chapter No. 6, Verse No. 7, that… 'Ant has got no ruler, no sear, no chief.' Today, we know that ants are sophisticated insects. They have a very good system of labour, in which they have chief, they have foreman and the workers. They even have a queen and a ruler. Therefore, the Bible is unscientific.

THE BIBLE SAYS THAT THE SERPENTS EAT DUST, IS NOT MENTIONED IN ANY GEOLOGICAL BOOK

Furthermore, it is mentioned in the Bible in Genesis, Chapter 3, Verse 14, and Isaiah Chapter 65, verse No. 25, that… 'Serpents eat dust.' No Geological book says 'Serpents eat dust.' It is mentioned in the Book of Leviticus, Chapter No.11, Verse No.20… 'Among the abomination things, fowls with four feet - They are an abomination.' And some scholars say that 'fowl' is a wrong translation of the Hebrew word 'uff.' In King James, it should be 'insect' or 'winged creature.' And in New International Version, it says… 'Winged creature.' But it says… 'All insects which are four-footed, are an abomination - They are detestful for you.'

I want to ask Dr. William Campbell… 'Which insects have got four feet?' Even a student, who has passed elementary school, knows that insects have got 6 feet. There is no bird in the world,

97

there is no foul in the world, and there is no insect in the world, which have got four feet. Furthermore, there are mythical animals and fabulous animals, which are mentioned in the Bible as though they exist - For example unicorn.

It is mentioned in the Book of Isaiah, Chapter 34, Verse No.7, talking about unicorn as though it exists. You look open the dictionary, it says... 'An animal which has got a horses' body, and a horn which is only available in myths.' My time is over; only I would like to tell that I apologise if I have hurt the feelings of any Christians. That was not my intention. It was just a reply to Dr. William Campbell's book to prove that the Qur'an is compatible with science. And the Bible, though a portion we do consider, may be the word of God, but the complete book is not the word of God - It is not in conciliation. And I would like to end my talk with the quotation of the Glorious Qur'an from Surah Isra Chapter.17, Verse No.81, which says: *'When truth is hurled against falsehood, falsehood perishes, for falsehood is by its nature bound to perish'*. Wa Aakhrudawana Anil Hamdulillahi Rabbil Aalameen.

QUESTION & ANSWER SESSION

Dr. Mohammed thanks Dr. William Campbell and Dr. Zakir Naik for their presentations as well as the response. He then announces for the beginning of the audience participation session, namely the Question & Answer session. At the same time, he makes it clear to all that the questions to be asked to Dr. Campbell and Dr. Zakir should be relevant and concerning the topic 'The Qur'an and the Bible : In the light of science'.

Question for Dr. Campbell: I would like to ask Dr. Campbell that in the Genesis, when it talks about the Noah's flood - it talks about the water that had covered the surface of the earth, all the creations and all the mountains and everything, and it says that it covered the highest mountain on earth, and that was 15 cubits, which is in Arabic, 15 foot you know 'kadam.' So we know scientifically that the highest mountain on earth is not 15 foot. You know it is a lot higher than that. So how come that in Genesis, it says that the water covered everything, every single mountain on earth - and the maximum height was 15 foot?

Dr. William Campbell: Thank you for your question. I think it is saying that it is above the highest mountain. If the highest mountain is 3000 meters, well then high ... it is 15 feet ... 15 foots above, it however. And then I looked into the Qur'an. I think it actually would be understood to be in the same way. Because, it says in Surah 11 Verse 40... 'The fountains of the earth gushed forth and the waves like mountains.' And then it says in the places where it gives a list of prophets - there is no prophet before Noah. And so I know Adam could be a Prophet, but I am.... So no where is it listed. And I think that it says in the Qur'an too, that the whole world was covered.

99

Question for Dr. Zakir Naik: You said, Allah reflects light and He is made of Nur - I could not really understand that. Could you explain that?

Dr. Zakir: The brother posed a question that he could not understand my explanation to the counter argument of Dr. William Campbell, regarding 'Nur' and 'Allah.' The Qur'an says in Surah Nur, Chapter 24, Verse No. 35, that Allah is 'Nurus samaavaati wal ardh' 'is the light' of the heavens and the earth – He is a light. The meaning of 'light' in the Qur'an is the 'reflected light' or borrowed light. So he is asking... 'Does it mean that even Allah has got borrowed light?' So the answer is given further, if you read the Verse - it says that it is like a parable of a niche - In the niche there is a lamp, which has a light of its own. That means Allah has light of His own and that light of His own is also being reflected.

The light of Allah Subhana-wa-taala is again being reflected by Allah himself like a halogen lamp that you see here. It has a tube in between. The lamp you can refer to that, as a 'Siraj' or a 'Wahaj' or a 'Dia' and the reflector as 'Munir' or 'Nur' borrowed light or 'reflection of the light.' And furthermore, but naturally this light - actually does not refer to the physical light you are talking about. It is a spiritual light of Allah Subhana-wa-taala. But as an answer, I have given to Dr. William Campbell. And since I have got 5 minutes, I would like to utilise it.

Dr. William Campbell gave a reply to Noah Alaihissalam. I am a person who use the concordance approach with the Bible, and conflict approach with the Qur'an, because both ways Alhamdullilah, the Qur'an will pass the test. And even if I agree with Dr. William Campbell, it is right, as it was 15 feet above the highest mountain. But it is mentioned in Genesis, Chapter No 7, Verse No 19 and 20, that... 'The full world was submerged under water.'

Furthermore, archaeological evidence show us today - and the time. Of Noah's time if you calculate by Genealogy, it comes to in the 21st to 22nd century B.C archaeological evidence show us today, that the 3rd Dynasty of Babylon, and the 11th Dynasty of Egypt were present at the 21st and 22nd century B.C, and there was no evidence of flood. They remained uninterrupted.

THE QUR'AN MATCHES WITH THE LATEST DISCOVERIES IN ARCHAEOLOGY BUT THE BIBLE DOES NOT

Therefore, archaeological evidences show us that it is impossible that the earth was submerged - the full earth was submerged under water in the 21st, 22nd century B.C What about the Qur'an? Point no 1 – the Qur'an does not give a date - whether 21st Century B.C. or 50th century B.C – No date is given therein. Point no 2 – Nowhere does the Qur'an say that the full world was submerged under water. It speaks about Noah Alaihissalam and his Qaum—his people. It was a small group of people or maybe a large group of people. Archaeological evidences tell today, and the Archaeologists say that... 'We have no objection – it is possible that parts of the world was submerged under water but submersion of the full world is not possible.' Thus, Alhamdulillah.The Qur'an is matching with the latest discoveries in Archaeology, but the Bible does not.

Furthermore, if you read Genesis, Chapter No 6, Verse No. 15 and 16, it speaks about Almighty God, telling Noah Alaihissalam to build an ark – giving it the length of 300 cubits, breadth 50

101

cubits and height 30 cubits. Cubit is 1 and a half feet - The brother made a mistake - it is one and a half feet. And the New International Version says... 450 feet in length and 75 feet in breadth, and approximately 45 feet in height - It is 30 cubit in height. I have done the calculation - it comes too less than 150 thousand cubic feet in volume and area-wise 33,750. And the Bible says there were 3 floors - Ground floor, 1st storey, and 2nd storey. So multiply by 3, you get an answer of 101 thousand, 250 square feet - That is the area.

Imagine a pair of all the species of the world was accommodated in 101 thousand and 250 square feet. Imagine! Is it possible? Millions of species are there in the world. If I tell... 'In this auditorium... one million people came in this auditorium'- Will you believe? I remember in the last year, I had given a talk in Kerala - and there were 1 million people. That was the biggest gathering I addressed, Alhamdulillah by Allah's grace. 1 million people! I could not see the end. It was not an auditorium - it was a big beach. I could not see any one - Only few people in the front. That is all. Few... compared to the one million people that were there. If you see on the videocassette, you will realise how big is one million – Somewhat like A'rafat - you see 2 ½ million people in A'rafat. In an area of 101 thousand, 250 square feet, or 150 thousand cubit feet, it is impossible - and above that, they stayed for 40 days eating, going for calls of the nature. If say...'1 million people came in this auditorium' - Will you believe? So scientifically, there are several things, in which there are gross scientific errors in the Bible.

Question for Dr. Campbell: Why do not you attempt the falsification test of the Bible, given in the book of Mark, Chapter.

16, Verses 17 and 18, and prove to the audience here right now, that you are a true Christian believer?

Dr. William Campbell: Well, I do not agree with Dr. Naik's interpretation. God... Jesus himself was tempted, and the devil said... 'If you are the Son of God, throw yourself off the temple.' And Jesus said... 'You will not tempt the Lord, your God. And so if I was on this day and say... 'Oh yes... I am going to be sure, and do a miracle in front of you' - I would be tempting God. My friend, Harry Rancliff had promised to go, and so he decided to keep his promise, and trust God to do His will. It is a different situation; I will not tempt God.

Question for Dr. Zakir: The Christians explain the concept of Trinity, scientifically by giving the example of water, which can be in 3 states - solid, liquid and gas, in the form of ice water and vapour. Similarly, one God is a Triune God – Father, son and Holy Ghost. Is this explanation scientifically correct?

Dr. Zakir Naik: Just a comment, before I give the answer - We should not tempt God... we should not test God. But here, we are not testing God; we are testing the human being. We are testing you and God promises that any believer, who has deadly poison, will not die - he will be able to speak in foreign tongues. We are not testing God, as we know that God is correct. He will see to it that every believer can speak. We are testing you, whether you are a believer or not.

Coming to the question, scientifically, I do agree that water can be in 3 forms solid, liquid and gas...Ice, water and vapour. But scientifically, we also know that the component of water remains the same. H_2O - 2 atoms of hydrogen, and one atom of oxygen. The components and constituents remain the same. Only the forms

103

keep on changing; there is no problem. Let's check with the Concept of Trinity – Father, Son, and Holy Ghost – Form… they say… 'Form changes.' Okay for the sake of argument, we agree. Does the component change? God and Holy Ghost are made of spirit - Human beings are made of flesh and bones - They are not the same.

Human beings require eating whereas God does not require eating to survive - They are not the same. And this is testified by Jesus Christ Peace be upon him, himself in the Gospel of Luke, Chapter No. 24, Verse No. 36 to 39. He says that… 'Behold my hands and feet - Handle me and see, for a spirit has no flesh and bones.' And he gave his hands, and they saw, and they were overjoyed. And he said that… 'Do you have any meat to eat?' And they gave him broiled fish and a piece of honeycomb, which he ate. To prove what? That he was God? It was to prove that he was not God. He ate, and he had flesh and bones while a spirit has got no flesh and bones. This proves that it is scientifically not possible that Father, Son and Holy Ghost - Father, Jesus Christ Peace be upon him, and Holy Ghost is Almighty God. And the concept of 'Trinity' - the word 'Trinity' does not exist anywhere in the Bible, but it is there in the Qur'an, which says in Surah Nisa, Chapter No. 4, Verse No. 171: 'Do not say trinity…desist stop it! It is better for you'. Trinity is also there in Surah Maidah, Chapter No.5, Verse No.73, which says… 'They are doing 'Kufr' - They are blaspheming - those who say that Allah in 3 in one - Is a triune God.

JESUS CHRIST (PBUH) NEVER SAID THAT HE WAS GOD

Jesus Christ Peace be upon him, never said that he was God. The concept of trinity does not exist in the Bible. The only verse closest

104

to the concept of 'Trinity' is the 1st Epistle of John, Chapter No.5, Verse No.7, which says... 'For there are three that bear record in heaven, the Father, the word and the holy ghost'. And these 3 are one. But if you read the Revised Standard Version, revised by 32 Christian scholars of the highest eminence backed by 50 different co-operative denominations, they say... 'This verse of the Bible - 1st Epistle of John, Chapter 5 Verse No.7 is an interpolation, a concoction and a fabrication' - It was thrown out of the Bible.

Jesus Christ Peace be upon him, never claimed Divinity. There is not a single unequivocal statement in the complete Bible, where Jesus Christ Peace be upon him, says... 'I am God' or where he says... 'Worship me'.

Infect if you read the Bible, it is mentioned in the Gospel of John, Chapter No.14, Verse No.28 – in which he said...'My Father is greater than I'. In Gospel of John, Chapter No.10, Verse No.29, he says, 'My Father is greater than all'. In Gospel of Mathew, Chapter No.12, Verse No.28, he says, 'I cast out devils with the spirit of God'; Gospel of Luke, Chapter No.11, Verse No.20...'I with the finger of God, cast out devil'; Gospel of John, Chapter No.5, Verse No.30... 'I can of my own self do nothing'...As I hear, I judge and my judgement is just, for I seek not my own will, but the will of my Father.'

JESUS CHRIST (PBUH) GAVE LIFE TO THE DEAD WITH GOD'S PERMISSION

Anyone who says... 'Not my will but God's will' is a Muslim. Muslim means the person who submits his will to the Almighty God. Jesus Christ Peace be upon him, said...'Not my will but God's will'.He was a Muslim, and he was Alhamdulillah, one of the mightiest messengers of God. We believe that he was born miraculously, without any male intervention. We believe he gave life to the dead with God's permission. We believe that he healed those born blind and the lepers with God's permission. We respect Jesus Christ Peace be upon him as one of the mightiest messenger of God. But he is not God, and he is not a part of the trinity that does not exist. The Qur'an says, 'Say He is Allah, One and Only.' Question for Dr. Campbell: The question is that we have come here together for this event tonight. It should benefit us. And so, I am asking Dr. Campbell. As a Christian and with your colleagues as well, has this event done its job - Has it opened your heart. Has it at least opened the glimmer towards looking further into the truth of Islam?

Dr. William Campbell: Well, I think I will use the last question to answer yours. Dr. Naik says… 'There is no place where Jesus says he is God.' In Mark 14:61, He did not answer - and again the high priest was questioning him, and saying to him… 'Are you the Christ, the son of the Blessed One?' In other words… 'Are you the Christ, the Son of God?' And Jesus said… 'I am'. So, he did say…'I am the Son of God, and he did say… 'He is Divine.' And the Bible clearly says. I realise Dr. Naik has quoted the verses, he wished to quote, where Jesus was in his human form. But there are other verses in which he says… 'I and the Father are one.' It says… 'In the beginning was the word, and the word was with God, and the word was God. And God was made flesh, and dwelt among us.'

In Jesus' baptism, the Father spoke and said… 'This is my beloved son.' Jesus was there, and the Holy Spirit descended - The Father, the Son and the Holy Spirit. We did not make this thing up from one head. Just ...a little thing - and now my friend asked the question here... 'We have learned many things', and I am always willing to learn. But I still think that the 500 witnesses that saw Jesus after he rose from the dead, have more power with me than Mohammed coming 600 years later as one witness - Thank you. Question for Dr. Zakir: Dr. Campbell did first attempt to bring up supposed false facts pertaining to the Qur'anic views on the universe, and you did refute these accusations.However, it was not addressed, what the Bible says about the shape of the earth, and those other aspects?

Dr. Zakir Naik: Sister asked the question that I did not address regarding what the Bible says about the shape of the earth. It was due to lack of time. I can point out another 100 points but lack of time is there. Anyhow, sister wants to know what the Bible speaks about shape of the earth.

It is mentioned in the Bible. In the Gospel of Mathew, Chapter No.4, Verse No.8, it says - the same reference which Dr. William Campbell used about tempting... 'The devil took him... (That is Jesus Christ, Peace be upon him) to an exceedingly high mountain, and showed him all the kingdoms of the earth and its glory'. The Gospel of Luke Chapter No.4, Verse No.5... 'The devil took him to a high mountain and showed him the glory of all the kingdoms of the world.'

THE BIBLE SAYS, THE EARTH IS FLAT

Now, even if you go to the highest mountain in the world i.e. Mount Everest and suppose you have a very good vision, and can see for thousands of miles together, yet, you will not be able to see all the kingdoms of the world. Because, today we know, the earth is spherical. You will not be able to see the kingdom of the opposite side of the world. The only way you will be able to see if the earth was flat. That is the description what the Bible gives…:'The earth is flat.'

THE 1ST CHRONICLES, CHAPTER NO.16, VERSE NO.30, SAYS, '*THE EARTH DOES NOT MOVE.*'

Furthermore, the same description is repeated in the book of Daniel, Chapter No.4, Verse No.10 and 11. It says… 'In a dream that the tree grew up into the heaven, and there when the tree grew up into the heaven, it grew up so much that every one from all the ends of the earth could see the tree'. This is only possible, if the shape of the earth was flat. If a tree is very long and the shape of the earth was flat, then it is possible. Today, it is a universal fact that the world is spherical. You will never be able to see the tree, however much long it is, from the opposite side of the spherical shape of the earth.

Besides, if you read, it is mentioned in the 1st Chronicles, Chapter No.16, Verse No.30, that… 'The earth does not move.' The same is repeated in the book of Psalms, Chapter No.93, Verse No.1, that… 'Almighty God has stabilised the earth.' That means the earth does not move. And in the New International Version, it says that… 'God has stabilised and stopped the movement of the earth as though…'

Dr. William Campbell said that Jesus Christ Peace be upon him said in the Bible at several places, that… 'He was God'. You can refer to my videocassette 'Concept of God in major Religions', which gives all the references and the answers. I will only give you the references of what he quoted… 'I and my Father are one' is from John, Chapter No 10, Verse No 30. And 'In the beginning was the word' from John Chapter No. 1, Verse No. 1. You go to the context, and you will come to know Jesus Christ Peace be upon him, never claimed Divinity. You can take my cassette, which is available at the foyer outside - 'Concept of God in major Religions', and 'Similarities between Islam and Christianity', which give the details that Jesus Christ Peace be upon him, never claimed Divinity.

Question for Dr. Campbell: You mentioned the test, where a true believer can drink poison, and survive because of their faith. What about ...Resputin, who was poisoned with enough cyanide, killed 16 people and when that did not kill him, he died of blood loss. He was not a good Christian - He had all this. How do you explain this? Well, only a good Christian can drink this poison and live - how do you explain that?

Dr. William Campbell: Well, I do not feel I have to explain it. I mean if Resputin was not a Christian, what happened to him has no basis for what happened in the Bible. I said before... Jesus... God did not intend for us to line up here, and start taking poisons, and sees whether he is the true God. Oh sorry! It was not to test God. That was given that God said that these things would happen. An example would be Paul - he went to... when he was shipwrecked - then he... I think it is Creep, but I have the wrong place in my mind - and he landed. And so, he was throwing wood into the fire and a snake bit him - Nothing happened to him. But he was not trying to test God - he was trying to throw wood on the fire. It is a different situation.

I would just like to say about the circle of the earth. In Isaiah 40:22, it says... 'He, God, sits enthroned above the circle of the earth.'

Question for Dr. Zakir: You said, there is not any mistake in the

Qur'an, but I see more than 20 mistakes in Arabic grammar, and I will tell you some of them. He said in Baqara. And Al-Haj… Which is right, Assabeun or Assabreen - Number 1. Number 2, you said…Of the same thing, he said in Surah Taha, 63…Mistake! Can you explain that? And there is more than that mistake.

Dr. Zakir: The brother has asked a very good question. I would like to be more concordant and agreeing. He has mentioned all 20 grammatical points. And the book he is referring to, by Abdul Faadi; is that correct? - Is the Qur'an infallible? I can see something… ya… Alhamdulillah my eyesight is good.

THE QUR'AN IS THE TEXTBOOK OF GRAMMAR, AND ALL ARABIC GRAMMAR HAS BEEN DERIVED FROM IT

Inshah-Allah, I will answer all 20 together, because I have read the book. Point No. 1 is to be noted that all Arabic grammar is taken from the Qur'an, which was the highest Arabic book - A book which has the maximum level of highest literature. All the Arabic grammar has been derived from the Qur'an, which is the textbook of grammar. Since the Qur'an is the textbook of grammar, and all the grammar is derived from the Qur'an, it can never have a mistake.

Point No. 2… It is like, you know… taking a ruler, and the ruler is there… has a measurement, and you are saying, the measurement is wrong - It sounds illogical. Point No. 2 - In the different tribes of Arabia, and you know Arabic, and Dr. William Campbell also will agree with me… In different Arabic tribes, the grammar keeps on changing. In some Arabic tribes, the word is feminine; the same word is even masculine in the other tribe. The same word in different tribes - the grammar keeps on changing. Even the gender

110

keeps on changing. So will you check the Qur'an with that faulty grammar? - No! And furthermore, the eloquence of the Qur'an is so high that it is far superior.

You know there are various books on the Internet. You go to 12 grammatical mistakes, 21 grammatical mistakes by Abdul Faadi – 20 grammatical mistakes. Do you think that the Christian people took out these mistakes? Do you know who took out these mistakes? The Muslims! The Muslim scholars like Zamak Sharif - what they did - that the Qur'anic grammar is so high that it goes against the conventional use of the Arabic. To prove the Qur'anic grammar was high, they gave examples. And I will give you a couple of examples, which will answer all his 20 questions. They gave the example - like we read in the Qur'an, it says that... 'The people of Lut (Alaihissalam) rejected all the messengers.' It is mentioned.

Dr. William Campbell said... 'The people of Noah rejected the messengers.' We know from history that there was only one messenger sent to them. So, it has a grammatical mistake. The Qur'an should have said - The people rejected the 'messenger' not 'messengers'. I agree with you - with layman grammar like how you and I know, it may be a mistake. But if you read the books written by Arabs - What is the beauty of the Qur'an? The beauty of the Qur'an is - Why does the Qur'an refer 'messengers' instead of 'messenger'? You know why? Because we know that the basic message of all the messengers was the same - That there is one God - About Tawheed - About Allah Subhana-wa-taala. By mentioning, the people of Lut Alaihissalam... the people of Noah rejected the messenger - It says, 'By rejecting Lut (Alaihissalam), they are indirectly rejecting all the messengers.'

111

See the beauty! See the eloquence... Alhamdulillah! You may think it is a mistake, but it is not a mistake. Similarly, people like Anis Shorrosh says, that Qur'an says... 'Qun fa ya Qun...Be and it is' - It should be 'Qun fa qaana' - 'Be and it was'. Past tense is Qun fa Qaana in Arabic – it is not Qun fa ya Qun. But the Qun fa ya Qun is more superior - It says... Allah - it was, it is, and can do - Past, present and future.

Question for Dr. Campbell: This is a very sincere question to learn a little more about Christianity. I want to ask that Jesus' Ministry was only for 3 years, after he was baptised by John the Baptist. So Jesus, the second most powerful person, after God... the son of God - what are his significant contributions in his early life from first one year to say 27 or 28 years? In the beginning of the presentation, Dr. Campbell mentioned Zulqarnain from the Chapter 18, of the Qur'an, 'The Cave' - and he mentioned that Zulqarnain is Alexander the great. Can you prove me, how you came to know that Zulqarnain is Alexander the great?

Dr. Campbell: I only read it in the commentary of Yusuf Ali. But regardless of whether it is Alexander the great or who it is, the sun does not set in a murky – marsh and that is what the verse says. Question for Dr. Zakir: (Q) I do not know the exact verse, but the Bible says... 'When Jonah was 3 days and 3 nights in the belly of the fish, so shall the son of man, be for 3 days and 3 nights in the heart of the earth.' Did Jesus Peace be upon him, scientifically fulfil the sign of Jonah?

Dr. Zakir: What the sister is referring to, is the verse of the Bible, Gospel of Mathew, Chapter No 12, Verse No. 38 and 40, when people asked Jesus Christ Peace be upon him... 'Show me a sign, show me a miracle'. Jesus Christ Peace be upon him, says... 'You evil and adulterations generation, seeketh after a sign, no sign shall be given to you, but the sign of Jonah. For as Jonah was 3 days and 3 nights in the belly of the whale, so shall the son of man be 3 days and 3 nights, in the heart of the earth' - Sign of Jonah.

Jesus Christ Peace be upon him, puts all his eggs in one basket. And if you go to the sign of Jonah... the book of Jonah is less than 2 pages, and most of us know. And if you analyse that Jonah was 3 days and 3 nights - but Jesus Christ Peace be upon him, we know from the Gospels that he was put on the cross - the alleged crucification. By late evening, he was brought down from the cross and put in a sepulchre - And on Sunday morning if you see, the stone is moved away, and the sepulchre is completely empty. So Jesus Christ Peace be upon him, is in the tomb, on Friday night.He was there in Saturday morning, one day, one night, one day and he was there on Saturday night - so two nights and one day - two nights. And Sunday morning the tomb was empty. So Jesus Christ Peace be upon him, was there for two nights, and one day - It is not 3 days and 3 nights.

Dr. William Campbell gives the reply in his book, that... 'You know, part of the day can be counted as one day – And if a patient comes to me, who is sick on Saturday night - on Monday morning, and if I ask him... 'How long are you sick for?' He will say... '3 days.' I agree with you - Concordance approach, I am very generous in this regard. You say part of the day is full day. So Saturday night, part of the day - one day. Sunday, part of the day, full day – one – good. Monday part of the day full day - No problem.

If patient says... '3 days' - No objection; but no patient will ever say... '3 days and 3 nights.' I challenge.I have Alhamdulillah met various patients - I have not come across a single patient, including Christian missionaries, who have ever told to me to be sick in the night, day before yesterday, saying... 'I am sick for 3 days, 3 nights.' So Jesus Christ Peace be upon him, did not say... '3 days' – He said... '3 days and 3 nights.' So, it is a mathematical error. Scientifically, Jesus Christ Peace be upon him, did not prove. And furthermore, the prophecy says... 'As Jonah was, so shall the son of man be.' How was Jonah in the belly of the Whale?... Belly of the fish... Dead or alive? Alive - When he was thrown overboard, he was alive. In the belly of the whale, he goes around the ocean, dead or alive? - Alive.He prays to Almighty God... dead or alive? - Alive! He is vomited out on the seashore - Dead of alive? Alive! When I ask the Christians... 'How was Jesus Christ Peace be upon him in the sepulchre... in the tomb - Dead or alive?'They tell me... 'Dead.'

JESUS CHRIST (PBUH) WAS NOT CRUCIFIED

The audience says, 'Alive'. Dr. Zakir resumes saying, 'Alive?' - Alhamdulillah! - Is it a Christian?If he is alive, Alhamdulillah, he was not crucified - If he is dead, he has not fulfilled the sign. You can refer to my videocassette 'Was Jesus Christ Peace be upon him really crucified?' I have proved that Jesus Christ Peace be upon him was not crucified. As the Qur'an says in Surah Nisa, Chapter 4, Verse No. 157...'They did not kill him, neither did they crucify him - It was only made to appear so.'

Question for Dr. Campbell: Dr. Campbell, since you are a medical doctor, could you please explain scientifically the various medical aspects that are given in the Bible, because you did not answer them in your rebuttal. For example, blood used as a disinfectant, Bitter Water Test for adultery, and most importantly, that the woman is unclean for double the period when she gives birth to a daughter than as compared to a son?

Dr. Campbell: Thank you for the question, and I will get to it. But Dr. Naik keeps getting the questions that shou'd come to the Christian. It says that… 'On the next day when it was one, after the preparation, the Chief Priest and the Phrases gathered together with Pilot.And said… 'Sir, we remember that when he was still alive, that he had said: After 3 days I am to rise again – Therefore, give waters for the grave to be made secure until the 3rd day. So they are using these words, interchangeably. As far as I am concerned, all of these word… 'The 3rd day, after the 3rd day, equal what happened with Jesus in the grave - The other thing is and then, his resurrection.There is one other thing - When Jesus was arrested, on Thursday night…

Thursday, and Thursday after… When he was arrested, he said… 'My hour has come.' And so I counted that 3 days and 3 nights. Now you have asked me about these places in the Bible. I believe that the Bible was written by God, and I believe that God put them in there. So it is not up to me to explain what God said, but I believe that God put those things in His Bible.

Question for Dr. Zakir: Assalaam alaikum. My name is Aslam Rauf, and I am a student studying Biology right now. And my teacher is teaching me… Evolution now - And I was wondering about the Islamic answer to 'Evolution' right now. If you could explain briefly - What Islam says on the topic of 'Evolution' and 'Creationism'.

Dr. Zakir: The brother has asked a question. Just as Dr. William Campbell is taking the liberty to answer; even I will take the liberty. Nowhere in the Qur'an is the name of 'Alexander' mentioned - It says 'Zulqarnain'… not 'Alexander.' If some commentator has made a mistake, it is a mistake in the commentary. The men have made the mistake - Not the word of God. Regarding the Bible, saying that… 'the world'…in Isaiah, 'is a circle.' No problem - It says… 'Circle', not spherical. So at one place, the Bible says… 'Flat'- one place it says... 'Circle'. If you agree to both the verses, it becomes like a disk. See - Does it look like the earth? It is circle, and it is flat - This is not the earth.

Regarding Biology in the Qur'an, and regarding 'Evolution' – the brother has asked two questions. I do not know whether I can answer both or not - I do not mind. Which answer do you want? First one, or the second one? – Biology? Or Evolution?

Two questions - Biology first, and then evolution. If you give me 10 minutes I will answer both. The exact answer, you can refer to my videocassette – 'The Qur'an and Modern Science.' When you talk about evolution, you start thinking about Darwin's theory. And Darwin went on his ship - at 'H.M.H. Bugle' to an island by the name of 'Calatropis' and he saw birds pecking at niches. Based on that observation that the beaks of the birds became long and short, he propounded the natural selection. But he wrote a letter to his friend, Thomas Thompton in 19th century in which he said that… 'I do not have proof to propound my natural selection but because it helped me in classification of embryology, of rudimentary organs, I put forth this.'

DARWIN'S THEORY HAS NO SCIENTIFIC PROOF

Darwin's theory is not a fact at all - It is only a theory. And I made it very clear in the beginning of my talk… 'The Qur'an can go against theories', because theories take U-turns, but the Qur'an will not go against any established fact. And in our school, we are

116

taught about Darwin's theory, as though it is a fact. It's not a fact. There is no scientific proof at all – 'there are missing links.' Therefore, if someone has to insult his friend or his colleague, he would say... 'If you were present at Darwin's time, Darwin's theory would have been proved right – insinuating he looks like an ape. There are missing links with Darwin's theory. And I know about the four fossils that are present - the Hominoids - the Lucy. Ortholopetians, with its guide, the Homoeructus, Naindertolman, and Cromageron – For details, refer to my videocassette. By molecular Biology, according to Hansis Cray, he said, it is impossible that we can be evolved from apes, by DNA coding - it is impossible. You can refer to my videocassette, which gives the details. In some parts, I have no objection.

Regarding Biology, the Qur'an says in Surah Ambiya, Chapter 21, Verse No. 30, ... 'We have created every living thing from water - Will you not then believe?' The basic substance... the cell contains cytoplasm, which has about 90% water. Every living creature in the world has approximately 50% to 90 % water. Imagine! In the deserts of Arabia, who could have imagined that everything is made of water? The Qur'an says that 14 hundred years ago.

Question for Dr. Campbell: If you cannot answer the contradictions in Genesis regarding the creation, don't you think that proves that the Bible is unscientific, and therefore not from God?

Dr. Campbell: I admit that I have some problems with this, but I also have all the fulfilled prophecies - and that is very important to me, and it says that... Jesus is the cornerstone, and built on a foundation of the apostles, so the Prophets prophesied and the

117

Apostles wrote down, when God fulfilled the prophecy. I know that does not answer your question, but my faith is in Christ as my saviour.

Question for Dr. Zakir: 'Text' and 'translations' are two different words, giving two different meanings in the Bible - in English language, 'a text' or 'a translation.' Cannot scientifically text and translation be proved to be the one and the same? Did God reveal His messages upon Moses and Jesus Peace be upon them, in English?

Dr. Zakir: It is a very good question - Can the text and the translation be the same? No! A 'text' and 'translation' cannot be exactly the same; they can come close to it. And according to Maulana Abdul Majid Dariabadi, the most difficult book in the world to translate is the Glorious Qur'an, because its language is so eloquent. It is so superior and noble - And one word in Arabic has got several meanings.

THE BIBLE WAS NOT REVEALED IN ENGLISH

Therefore to translate the Qur'an, is the most difficult - It is not the same. And if there is a mistake in the translation, it is a human handiwork - the human being who is translating is to be blamed, not the Almighty God. Regarding - Was Bible revealed in English? No! The Bible was not revealed in English. Its Old Testament is in Hebrew while the New Testament is in Greek.

JESUS CHRIST (PBUH) SPOKE HEBREW

Though Jesus Christ Peace be upon him, spoke Hebrew, the original manuscript that you have, is in Greek. The Old Testament, the original Hebrew is not available. Do you know that? The Hebrew translation of the Old Testament is from the Greek. So even the original Old Testament, which in Hebrew is not present in Hebrew.

118

THE ORIGINAL ARABIC IS MAINTAINED IN THE QUR'AN

So, you have a double problem - No wonder you have scribal errors etc., but Alhamdulillah, the original Arabic is maintained in the Qur'an. It has been... Alhamdulillah scientifically proved, you can prove it as the same. And regarding - Were Revelations revealed to Jesus Christ Peace be upon him, and to Moses Peace be upon him? I said in my earlier answers as well as my talk that we believe in the Qur'an which says in Surah Al-Rad, Chapter. 13, Verse 38, that Allah Subhan-wa-taala has sent down several Revelations.By name only 4 are mentioned - The Torah the Zaboor, the Injeel and the Qur'an.

THE PRESENT BIBLE IS NOT THE INJEEL

The Torah is the Wahi, which was given to Moses, Peace be upon him. The Zaboor is the Revelation, the Wahi which was given to David, Peace be upon him. The Injeel is the Revelation, Wahi which was given to Jesus, Peace be upon him. And the Qur'an is the last and final Revelation which was given to the last and final Messenger, Prophet Mohammed, May peace be upon him.But the present Bible is not the Injeel, which we believe in and which was revealed to Jesus Christ, Peace be upon him.

Dr. Campbell: But the present Injeel is the one as always been. We have .75 percent of the texts from 180 A.D - That is 100 years after John wrote. He was alive, and wrote. You have the people alive at that point, who knew whom their grandparents believed through John. That is a good evidence, and good text - The Bible is a valid history. Now the question - With the probability you presented is a great calculation - Thank you. But in the matter of God, it is completely inferior. God is All Powerful, and can choose who he likes.' Of course no matter rich or poor or any other thing - so how then does your probability fit in? Jesus was poor - he was chosen. He said… 'The son of man has no where to lay his head.' I am not sure about this – I do not see how the calculation is talking about that. Calculation was as to how many people could fulfil all those prophecies. I hope that's been helpful - Thank you.

Question for Dr. Zakir: To an effort to prove that the Qur'an is so heavily agreeable to modern science - what happens if the modern science is wrong? Does the Qur'an always change to reflect the changes in science?

Dr. Zakir: It is a very good and important question. And we the Muslims should be very careful while being compatible with the Qur'an and modern science. Therefore, I said in the beginning of my talk - I will only be speaking about those scientific facts, which have been established. And a scientific fact, which has been established - for example, the earth is spherical - It can never go wrong. Established science can never take U-turns. But unestablished science like hypothesis and theories can take U-turns.

THE QUR'AN NEVER GOES AGAINST THE ESTABLISHED SCIENTIFIC PROOFS

I know some of the Muslim scholars, who have tried to prove Darwin's theory from the Qur'an. Nonsense! So therefore, we should not go overboard, and try and prove everything of modern science. We have to be careful to check up whether it is established or unestablished. If it is established, Alhamdulillah with scientific proof, the Qur'an will never go against it. If it is hypothesis, it may be right, it may be wrong; like the 'Big Bang' theory, which was a hypothesis earlier. Today, after solid proof about the celestial matter… according to Steven Hawkins etc., it is a fact. So today, the Big Bang theory is a fact while yesterday (earlier) it was a hypothesis. Once it becomes a fact, I use it.

You know there is the hypothesis, saying that… 'Human beings have been created from a single pair of genes' - Adam and Eve. I do not use it, because science has not established. It goes along with the Qur'an that we have been evolved from one pair—Adam and Eve, Peace be upon them but I do not use it, because that is not an established fact.

Therefore, while bringing a co-relation between the Qur'an and science etc., see to it that you use only those scientific facts which have been established… and not hypothesis, because the Qur'an is far superior to modern science. I am not trying to prove the Qur'an to be the word of God, with the help of science – No, not at all. What I am trying to do - For us the Muslims, the Qur'an is the ultimate criteria - For the Atheist and for the Non-Muslims, science may be the ultimate criteria. I am using the criteria… the yardstick of the Atheists, and comparing it with the yardstick of the Muslims i.e. the Holy Qur'an.

I am not trying to prove the Qur'an to be the word of God with the help of science. What I am trying to do is, when I bring a compatibility, I show the superiority of the Qur'an, and that is what your science has told us yesterday, but the Qur'an has told us 14 hundred years ago. I am trying to prove that our yardstick or the Muslims' yardstick… the Qur'an is far superior to your yardstick - the science. Therefore, you should believe in the Qur'an, which is far superior - Hope that answers the question.

Question for Dr. Campbell: Dr. Campbell agreed with Dr. Naik that the errors he showed are not wrong, and that he cannot answer them. So, does this mean that Dr. Campbell agrees that the Bible has errors, and so, it is not the word of God?

Dr. Campbell: There are things in the Bible that I cannot explain - that I do not have an answer for now. And I am willing to wait until I see whether an answer comes. There are many places where archaeological things have proved the Bible true - talking about towns, who is the king, and things like that. And I think there is great proof that the Bible is valid in good history.

Question for Dr. Zakir: The question is... 'Are there any more mathematical contradictions in the Bible?' Are there any more mathematical contradictions in Islam? Is it the Bible or Islam? - I do not know.

Dr. Zakir: I will answer both. Because... 'Is there any more?' - It should be the Bible, because I spoke about contradictions. Anyway, regarding Islam, the Qur'an says in Surah Nisa, Chapter 4, Verse No.82... 'Do they not consider the Qur'an with care? - Had it been from anyone besides Allah, there would have been many contradictions.' There is not a single. Regarding more contradictions in the Bible - five minutes will be insufficient to say. Even if they give me 5 days' time, then also it will be difficult. Anyway, I will just mention a few.

It is mentioned in the 2nd Kings, Chapter No.8, Verse No.26, it says that... 'Ahezia was 22 years old, when he began to reign.' 2nd Chronicles, Chapter No. 22, Verse No. 2, says that... 'He was 42 years old, when he began to reign'. Was he 22 years old or 42 years old? It's a mathematical contradiction. Furthermore, in 2nd Chronicles, Chapter No. 21, Verse No. 20, it says that... 'Joaram, the father of Ahezia reigned at the age of 32 - and he

122

reigned for 8 years, and he died at the age of 40. Immediately...
Ahezia became the next ruler at the age of 42. Father died at the
age of 40 - Immediately son takes over, who is at the age of 42'.
How can a son be two years older than the father? Believe me,
even in Hollywood film, you will not be able to produce it.
In Hollywood film, you can produce a 'unicorn' which I mentioned
in my talk. Unicorn... you can have Concrodyasis, which the Bible
speaks about, Concrodyasis and dragons and serpents. But in
Hollywood you cannot even show a son, being two years older
than the father. It cannot even be a miracle. Even in miracles, it is
not possible. In miracle, you can have a person being born of a
virgin birth, but you cannot have a son being older than the father
by 2 years.

Further, if you read, you'll find in the Bible in 2nd Samuel Chapter
No 24, Verse No 9, says that... 'The people that were involved
in the battlefield who took part were 800 thousand of the men of
Israel, took part - and 500 thousand of the men of Judah same.' If
you see other places, 1st Chronicle, Chapter 21, Verse No. 5, it
says that... '1 million - Hundred thousand people took part in the
battlefield, from the men of Israel - and ten thousand four hundred
and sixty men took part of Judah.' Was it 800 thousand people
who took part from the men of Israel or was it 1 million - 100
thousand? Was it 5 lakh people of Judah that took part or 10,460?
It's a clear-cut contradiction.

Furthermore, it is mentioned in the Bible in 2nd Samuel, Chapter
No. 6, Verse No 23, that... 'Michael the daughter of Saul had no
sons' - 2nd Samuel', Chapter 21, Verse No. 8... 'Michael the
daughter of Saul had 5 sons.' One place it says... 'No children,
no son, no daughter' - Other place... '5 sons.' Furthermore, if

123

you read, it is mentioned in Gospel of Mathew, Chapter No. 1, Verse No. 16 - it says about the genealogy of Jesus Christ Peace be upon him, and Luke Chapter No. 3, Verse No. 23 says that... 'Jesus' father (that is Joseph) was Jacob' – Mathew, Chapter 1, Verse 16. And Luke, Chapter No 3, Verse No 23... 'Jesus' father (Joseph) was Hailey'. Did Jesus' father (Joseph) have two fathers? What do you call a person who has got two fathers? Or was it Hailey or was it Jacob? It is a clear-cut contradiction.

CONCLUSION

Finally, Dr. Sabeel Ahmed concludes the programme, saying: On behalf of the Islamic Circle of North America, I would really thank all of you for your patience and all our distinguished guests over here for giving up a very good performance for all of us.

***

124